Copycat Recipes

How to Prepare the Most Popular Dishes from Restaurants at Home
(2022 Copycat Cookbooks for Beginners)

Bruno Hansen

CONTENT LIST

Introduction

Everyone enjoys dining out once in a while, whether it's a date night with their significant other, a family dinner at a nice restaurant, lunch out, or coffee. With friends at a nearby café, or even a quick stop at a favorite fast-food restaurant place. There's just something about dining out, whether alone or with Others. The Company makes eating even more enjoyable. Perhaps you believe you'll never be able to replicate the food at Outback Steakhouse. Starbucks, Chipotle, or Applebee's So you go in, stand in line for what seems like an eternity, and then pay for food you know is way overpriced. But what if you didn't have to endure all of that? What if...You could be eating your favorite dessert that you made right in your own home. Home? There will be no leaving the house, no waiting in lines, and no spending of money. Expensive food—just the incredible taste of your favorite restaurant dishes and the satisfaction that you were able to recreate them all on your own (or with the help of others).together with friends or family). And, with the assistance of this cookbook, you will be able to accomplish this in no time. The primary goal of this Copycat series is to bring you tried-and-true recipes that taste exactly like the ones in your favorite restaurants restaurant.

This is the second cookbook in the series. You will find it in it. Find even more of your favorite recipes from popular restaurants. From all over the United States.

The Price of Eating Out

When you pay for a meal at a restaurant, you are usually paying three times the cost of the ingredients used to prepare the food. That's Around $14 in a restaurant, which would have cost $4.25 if you had brought your own. You did it yourself. There are four methods for restaurant owners to price their menu. Items. The first method is based on the following equation: "cost of raw materials. "Divided by "desired food cost percentage (approximately 25-30%)" equals "the cost." This is how the $14 restaurant meal cost was determined previously. The second approach is to base the price on the prices of competing restaurants. Restaurant owners will either charge the same price as their competitors, or they will charge a higher price. Lower their meal prices for those looking for a better deal, or raise When compared to their competitors, their prices appear to be of higher quality. The third menu pricing method is to base prices on supply and demand. Food, for example, is typically more expensive in places such as sports stadiums. And airports because they know you'll be hungry or thirsty.

And there aren't many alternatives. Restaurants with distinct themes to their interior or food can also raise their prices as a result of the Customers are not only paying for the food but also the overall experience. Dining encounter Finally, the fourth and final pricing method is to assess your menu. Profitability of items If restaurant owners are aware that one particular meal is popular, If they sell well, they will raise the other prices by a small, insignificant amount. Amount so that it can compete with the best-sellers in terms of profitability When you eat at a restaurant, regardless of the pricing method, you're paying. Not only for the food but also for the restaurant's overhead This cookbook contains even more copycat recipes from your favorite restaurants. Restaurants that can be made at home in as little as 30 minutes. There Over 100 recipes are ranging from breakfast to snacks to entrees. There are a variety of sides and desserts to choose from. You'll begin to cook like a restaurant chef. Quickly become a chef!

Chapter 1

Copycat Breakfast Recipes

IHOP's Buttermilk Pancake

IHOP pancakes have always had a distinctive flavor. If you're looking for a quick and delicious breakfast, here's a recipe that will satisfy your taste buds 8 to 10 servings – Preparation Time: 5 minutes – Preparation Time: 8 minutes

Nutritional information per serving: Calories: 180.1, Total Fat: 7.9 g, Carbohydrates: 23.2 g 4.1 g protein, 271.6 mg sodium

Ingredients

- 1 14 cups all-purpose flour
- 1 tsp. baking soda
- 1 tsp. baking powder
- 1 pound granulated sugar

- ONE EGG
- 1 14 cups buttermilk
- 14 c.o

Preparation

- Preheat your pan by leaving it on medium heat while you prepare the other ingredients. making the pancake batter
- Combine all of your dry ingredients in a mixing bowl.
- Combine all of your wet ingredients in a mixing bowl.
- Carefully fold the dry mixture into the wet mixture until it is completely incorporated.
- Everything is completely mixed. Melt some butter in a skillet.
- Pour the batter into the pan in a slow, circular motion until you have a 5-inch circle.
- Flip the pancake when the edges appear to be hardening.

- Cook the pancake on the other side until golden brown.
- Continue with steps 6–8 until your batter is finished.
- Drizzle with softened butter and maple syrup to serve.

Breakfast Burrito at McDonald's

TO ROUND OUT YOUR MORNING ROUTINE, MAKE A SIMPLE MCDONALD'S BURRITO.

10 servings – 10 minutes to prepare – Preparation Time: 16 minutes

Nutritional information per serving: Calories: 270.1, Total Fat: 14.8 g, Carbohydrates: 18.2 g Sodium 525.3 mg, 15.2 g protein

Ingredients

- 12 pound cooked and crumbled bulk sausage
- 10 scrambled eggs

- 1 medium diced tomato
- 3 tbsp. diced canned green chilia pinch of salt and pepper 10 warm flour tortillas10 halved slices of American cheesea little salsaa little sour cream

Preparation

- In a medium-sized mixing bowl, combine the first six ingredients.
- Melt butter in a nonstick skillet over medium heat.
- Pour the mixture into the pan and cook until the egg is cooked through.
- Cooked to your liking
- When the mixture has reached the desired consistency, remove it from the heat turn off the heat
- Begin assembling your burritos by laying out the tortillas.
- Each tortilla should contain one-tenth of the mixture.
- Place the cheese on top of the egg mixture and roll up the tortilla.
- To make the burrito, use a tortilla.
- To serve, top the roll with salsa and sour cream

Marble Pound Cake from Starbucks

Sugar is sometimes required to get the blood pumping in the morning. Make this pound cake the night before and enjoy a slice before heading to bed. work. 16 servings – 10 minutes to prepare – Preparation Time: 1 hour 30 minutes Nutritional information per serving: Calories: 582.1, Total Fat: 32 g, Carbohydrates: 69.6 g Sodium 114.8 mg, 8.6 g protein

Ingredients

- 420 g cake flour
- 2 teaspoons baking soda
- 18 teaspoon of salt
- 6 ounces finely chopped semisweet chocolate
- 2 cups softened unsalted butter

- granulated sugar 3 cups
- 1 tablespoon vanilla extract
- 1 lemon, grated, grated for zest
- ten large eggs
- 2 tbsp orange liqueur OR milk

Preparation

- Gather your ingredients and then:
- Preheat the oven to 350 degrees Fahrenheit;
- Grease a 104-inch tube pan with cooking spray;
- Line the bottom of the pan with greased wax paper; and Flour the entire baking dish.
- In a medium-sized mixing bowl, sift together the cake flour, baking powder, and salt.This is your dry mixture in a bowl.
- In a medium-sized mixing bowl, melt the chocolate and then beat in the butter. When the mixture is smooth, add the sugar, lemon zest, and vanilla extract and vanilla extract until the liquid mixture is homogeneous.

- Once the mixture has been thoroughly beaten, add the eggs, two at a time until the mixture appears curdled
- Combine half of your dry mixture with half of your liquid mixture. Until well combined
  - Stir in the orange liquor and the remaining dry ingredients. Continue whirling the mixture
  - When the mixture is well combined, begin folding it with a spatula—Here's your batter.
  - 8 Reserve 4 cups of the batter. In a mixing bowl, combine the melted chocolate and the remainder of the batter
  - Now that you have a light and a dark batter, combine them.
  - Spoonfuls of batter into the tube pan, alternating between the two different colors
  - When the pan is full, gently shake it to level the batter. Execute a to marble the batter, run a knife through it.
  - Bake for 1 hour and 15 minutes in a baking pan. Poke the cake with a toothpick to see if it's done.

there are any, when you remove the toothpick, there are still some moist crumbs on tithe cake is then finished.

- 12 Remove the cake from the pan and set it aside to cool overnight.

Scrambled Egg at IHOP

Scrambled eggs are a traditional breakfast item. This dish is simple but delicious. A delectable upgrade to your standard breakfast eggs.

servings – 5 minutes to prepare – Preparation Time: 5 minutes

Nutritional information per serving: 870 calories Carbohydrates 9 g, Total Fat 54 g69 g protein, 34.9 mg sodium

Ingredients

- 14 cup pancake batter
- 12–14 tbsp. butter six large eggs.Season with salt and pepper to taste.
- Preparation
- Thoroughly combine the pancake mix and eggs until no lumps remain.
- There are still lumps or clumps.
- Melt butter in a skillet over medium heat.
- When the pan is hot enough, pour in the egg mixture. in the pan

- Season with salt and pepper and set aside for about a minute.
- When the egg begins to cook, begin pushing the edges of the
- Move the mixture to the center of the pan. Continue until all of the
- The mixture has been cooked.
- Plate and serve.

Fruit and Yogurt Parfait from McDonald's

There's no need to go to McDonald's to get that delicious fruit and yogurt parfait.Make one at home and consume it before beginning your day.

10 servings – 5 minutes to prepare – Preparation Time: n/a

Nutritional information per serving: Calories: 328.9, Total Fat: 25.4 g, Carbohydrates: 20.7 g

Sodium 79.7 mg, protein 9 g

Ingredients

6 ounces vanilla yogurt (divided into 3 portions)

- 4–6 sliced strawberries
- 14 cup fresh or frozen blueberries, divided
- 14 cup chopped pecans, divided into two

Preparation

- Put 2 ounces of vanilla yogurt in the bottom of a cup, then pour in the rest of the ingredients.
- 2–3 strawberries, 18 cup blueberries, and 18 cup pecans
- Add another layer of yogurt, strawberries, blueberries, and raspberries.
- On top of the first layer, sprinkle with pecans.
- Finish the parfait with the remaining yogurt—you can garnish if desired.
- You can top it with more fruits if you want.

Cinnamon Crunch Bagel from Panera Bread

This bagel can be made at any time and eaten on the go or right before you goes to bed.

Get out of the house. Make a restaurant-quality breakfast at home!

Serves 8 – Prep Time: 1 Hour – Cook Time: 25 Minutes

Nutritional information per serving: 463 calories Carbohydrates 71 g, Total Fat 16 g

6 g protein, 296 mg sodium

Ingredients

- Bread:
- 14 cup warm water (between 110 and 120 degrees Fahrenheit)
- 1 teaspoon yeast
- 1 teaspoon salt
- 4 tbsp honey (distributed)
- 112.25 cup whole wheat pastry flou
- 12 teaspoon cinnamon
- 1 pound bread flour a quarter cup white chocolate chips
- For sprinkling, use cornmeal.
- 414 quarts of water
- Topping:
- 14 cup sugar, granulated
- 14 cup brown sugar, packed
- 14 teaspoon cinnamon
- 1 / 3 cup coconut oil

Preparation

- Activate the yeast by combining it with warm water and allowing it to sit for a few minutes set aside for 10 minutes
- Mix in 3 tablespoons of honey, salt, pastry flour, and the ground cinnamon With a dough mixer, combine all of the ingredients a wooden spoon or a mixer After about a minute of mixing, or when the
- When all of the flour has been incorporated, scrape down the sides of the bowl and continue to mix once more for a few minutes
- Allow the dough to rest for 5 minutes—if lumps form, stir the batter to remove them.Separate them.
- Begin kneading with half a cup of bread flour. Continue to add while adding half a cup of bread flour at a time until finished kneading the dough to distribute the flour evenly
- Add the white flour after about seven minutes of kneading.

- Continue kneading until the chocolate chips are completely incorporated.
- Incorporate the chips into the mixture.
- Cover the bowl with a towel and set aside the dough for one hour hour.
- After an hour, flour a flat surface on which to set your dough. Remove the dough from the

  bowl and place it on a floured surface and knock it down.
- Divide the dough into eight equal pieces. Make ropes out of them. Allow the
- Allow the dough to rest for another 3 to 4 minutes.
- Twist the ends of each piece of dough to form a circle securely joined Cornmeal should be sprinkled on a baking sheet.
- Layout the dough circles on the baking sheet. Allow drying after covering with a towel.
- Take a 10- to 15-minute break.

- Prepare your materials while the dough is resting by:
- (1)Bring the water to a rolling boil. When the water begins to boil, add the
- 1 tablespoon remaining honey Maintain a low boil in the water;
- (2)Preheat the oven to 450 degrees Fahrenheit.
- (3)Place parchment or wax paper on a baking sheet; and
- (4)Combine the topping ingredients (except the oil).
- After 15 minutes, immerse a few dough circles in the boiling water. Cook them for 50 seconds on each side. When it comes to
- After the bagels have boiled, place them on a baking sheet with a spatula using a slotted spoon to drain the water
- After all of the bagels have boiled, brush them all with coconut oil and then sprinkling with the sugar mixture

- Bake your bagels for 20 to 25 minutes before transferring them to a cooling rack to cool on a wire rack

Chocolate Cinnamon Bread from Starbucks

If you want something sweet to start your day, this delicious chocolate bread might be just what you're looking for. 16 servings – 15 minutes to prepare – Preparation Time: 1 Hour Nutritional information per serving: 370 calories Total Fat 14 g, Carbohydrates 59 g Sodium 270 mg, protein 7 g

Ingredients

- Bread:
- 12-pound unsalted butter
- granulated sugar 3 cups
- 5 extra-large eggs
- 2 c. flour

- 114 cup cocoa (processed)
- 1 tablespoon cinnamon powder
- 1 teaspoon sea salt
- 12 tsp baking powder
- 12 tsp baking soda
- 14 cups of water
- 1-quart buttermilk
- 1 tsp vanilla extract
- Topping:
- 14 cup sugar, granulated
- 12 teaspoon ground cinnamon
- 12 teaspoon cocoa (processed)
- 18 teaspoon ground ginger
- 18 teaspoon ground cloves

Preparation

- Before you begin cooking:
- Preheat the oven to 350 degrees Fahrenheit;

- Lightly grease two 953 loaf pans; and
- Line the pan bottoms with wax paper.
- Beat the sugar and butter together to make a cream.
- Add the eggs, one at a time, to the mixture.
- Combine the flour, cocoa, cinnamon, salt, baking powder, and baking soda in a mixing bowl.
- Pour the soda into a large mixing bowl.
- In a separate bowl, combine the water, buttermilk, and vanilla.
- 6. Make a well in the dry ingredients and begin pouring in the wet.
- while whisking the mixtures a little at a time
- 7. When the mixture begins to become doughy, divide it in half and set it aside.
- 8. Combine all of the topping ingredients and sprinkle evenly on top. in both pans, on top of
- 9. Bake for 50–60 minutes, or until the bread is

Lemon Loaf from Starbucks

Lemon loaves are both energizing and refreshing. Take a bite of Before you start your day, treat yourself to a Starbucks-style lemon loaf. 8

servings – 15 minutes to prepare – Preparation Time: 45 minutes

Nutritional information per serving: Calories: 425.2, Total Fat: 18.7 g, Carbohydrates: 60 g

5 g protein, 310.8 mg sodium

Ingredients

- Bread:
- 1 12 cup flour
- 12 tsp baking soda
- 12 tsp baking powder
- 12 teaspoon of salt
- 1 cup of sugar
- 3 room temperature eggs
- 2 tablespoons softened butter
- 1 tsp vanilla extract
- 1 / 3 cup lemon juice
- 12 cup olive oil
- Icing:
- 1 cup plus 1 tbsp powdered sugar
- two tbsp milk
- 12 tsp lemon extract
- Preparation
- Prepare your baking materials by:
- Preheat the oven to 350°F;
- Grease and flour a 953 loaf pan; and
- Line the bottom of the pan with wax paper.
- In a large mixing bowl, combine the first four

ingredients—this is your dry mixture.

- In a mixing bowl, combine the eggs, butter, vanilla, and lemon juice until the mixture is smooth in a medium mixing bowl This is your opportunity a wet mixture
- Make a well in the center of the dry mixture and pour in the wet mixture fill the well with the mixture
- Combine everything with a whisk or a hand
- Add the crude oil Do not stop mixing until everything is completely combined and smooth.
- Pour the batter into the pan and bake for 45 minutes—the bread will be done.
- When you can stick a toothpick into it and it comes out clean, it's done clean.
- While the bread is baking, prepare the icing by combining the icing ingredients.
- Using a whisk or a hand mixer, combine all of the ingredients in a small bowl smooth.
- Remove the bread from the oven and place it on a cooling rack to cool.

- Allow it to cool for at least 20 minutes.
- When the bread is cool enough to handle, spread the icing on top. Wait before slicing, allow the icing to set.

The Waffle House Waffle

Nothing beats a good waffle to get your day started. If you have a craving, Here's a recipe that will satisfy your craving for those delectable Waffle House waffles Those desires. 6 servings – 5 minutes to prepare – Preparation Time: 20 minutes Nutritional information per serving: Calories 313.8, Fat 12.4 g, Carbohydrates 45 g

5.9 g protein, 567.9 mg sodium

Ingredients

- 1 12 cups all-purpose flour
- 1 teaspoon sea salt

- 12 tsp baking soda
- ONE EGG
- 12 cup granulated white sugar + 1 tablespoon
- 2 tablespoons softened butter
- 2 tbsp. vegetable shortening
- 12 c. half-and-half
- a 12 cup milk
- 14 cups of buttermilk
- 14 teaspoon vanilla extract

Preparation

- Make the dry mixture by sifting the flour into a bowl and whisking it together.
- combining it with the baking soda and salt
- Lightly beat an egg in a medium mixing bowl. When the egg has matured
- When the mixture is frothy, add butter, sugar, and shortening. When it comes to
- When the mixture is thoroughly combined, add half-and-half, vanilla, and salt. buttermilk and milk Continue to beat the mixture until it is smooth smooth.

- Slowly pour in the dry mixture while beating the wet mixture. ensuring thorough mixing and removal of all lumps
- Chill the batter overnight (optional, but recommended; if you don't have a refrigerator).
- If the mixture cannot be chilled overnight, leave it for at least 15 to 20 minutes. s).
- Remove the battery from the refrigerator. Preheat your oven and grease it. waffle maker
- Cook each waffle for three to four minutes on each side. Serve with butter and lemon. syrup.

Omelet at Mimi's Café Santa Fe

Here's another egg recipe to get you started in the morning. Serve this on a plate. Start your day right with a scrambled omelet. 1 serving – 10 minutes to prepare – Preparation Time: 10 minutes Nutritional information per serving: 519 calories, 32 g total fat, 60 g carbs

14 g protein, 463 mg sodium

Ingredients

- Chipotle Aioli:
- 1 cup tomato sauce or marinara
- 34 cups of water
- 12 cup adobo-spiced chipotle

- 1 tsp. kosher salt
- Omelet:
- 1 tablesoon diced onions
- 1 tablespoon diced jalapenos
- 2 tbsp. cilantro, chopped
- 2 tablespoons diced tomatoes
- 14 cup fried corn tortillas, sliced
- 3 beaten eggs
- 2 cheese slices
- 1 tsp salt and pepper
- Garnish:
- 2 oz. hot chipotle sauce
- 14 cup fried corn tortillas, sliced
- 1 tbsp. green onions, sliced
- 1 teaspoon guacamole

Preparation

- Melt some butter in a pan over medium heat, being careful not to burn it. the entire skillet
- Saute the jalapenos, cilantro, tomatoes, onions, and tortilla strips in a skillet over medium heat. for approximately one minute

- Season the eggs with salt and pepper and stir them in occasionally.
- When the omelet has been set, flip it. Place the cheese on the top half of the pan.
- Fold the omelet in half when the cheese begins to melt and place on a plate
- Top the omelet with chipotle sauce, guacamole, green onions, and cilantro as well as corn tortillas.

Chapter 2

Copycat Recipes for Snacks and Side Dishes

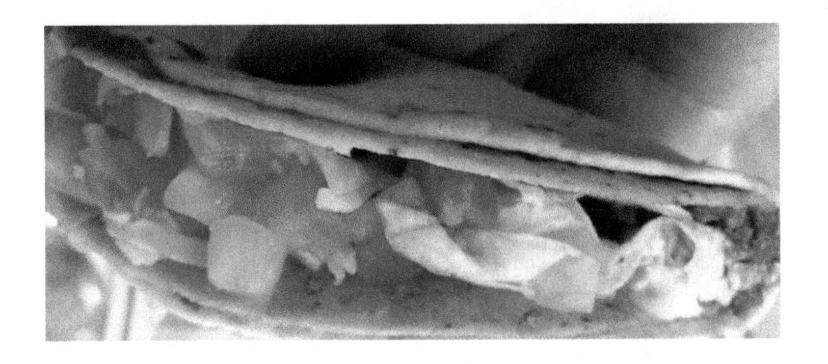

Double Decker Tacos from Taco Bell

Tacos are a fantastic snack. Have a Taco Bell Double Decker Taco to go with it fulfill your cravings 10 servings – 30 minutes to prepare – Preparation Time: 15 minutes

Nutritional information per serving: 485 calories Carbohydrates 37.3 g, Total Fat 26.3 g

Sodium 741 mg, 18.9 g protein

Ingredients

- Taco:
- 1 pound minced beef
- 1-ounce taco seasoning mix (distributed)
- 1 tin (16 oz.) refried beans
- 13 cups of water
- 12 taco shells, crisp

- To serve, sour cream
- Guacamole:
- two avocados
- 2 tbsp. chopped onions
- 1 lime, freshly squeezed
- To taste, season with salt and black pepper.
- Assembling:
- 12 soft flour tortillas (approximately 7-inch diameter)
- 2 cups cheddar cheese, shredded
- 1 cup lettuce, shredded
- 1 large tomato, diced
- 14 chopped red onion
- 12 cup soured cream
- To taste, season with salt and black pepper.

Preparation

- Preheat the oven to 350 degrees Fahrenheit.
- Cook the beef for 10 to 15 minutes over medium heat, sprinkling with salt and pepper. it with 34 ounces taco seasoning When the beef has turned brown

- Remove from the heat when it's crumbly and set aside. Season the remaining taco seasoning mix over the refried beans. by combining the beans, water, and seasoning in a small pot and bringing to a boil combining and mashing everything Mash the beans and set them aside
- Bring the mixture to a low boil.
- Preheat the taco shells for 3 to 5 minutes in the oven.
- Prepare the guacamole while the taco shells are heating. combining all of the guacamole ingredients
- Begin assembling the tacos by covering one side of each flour tortilla.
- Wrapping the tortilla with 2 tablespoons of the bean mixture a flour tortilla wrapped around a taco shell Then insert the following by the taco
- 2 tbsp. ground beef
- 2 tbsp. grated cheese
- Lettuce shreds
- Tomato and onion, chopped
- On the side, serve with guacamole and sour

Stuffed Bread from Domino's

Domino's is well-known not only for its pizza but also for its stuffed bread. It's the ideal combination of crispy and chewy that will satisfy all of your cravings guests. 6 servings – 10 minutes to prepare – Preparation Time: 25 minutes

Nutritional information per serving: 420 calories Carbohydrates 25.7 g, Total Fat 26.5 g Sodium 810 mg, 19.4 g protein

Ingredients

- 1 package (11 ounces) refrigerated French bread
- 4 tbsp melted butter (divided)
- 1 teaspoon cornmeal
- 1 cup mozzarella cheese, shredded

- 1 cup Mexican cheese blend, shredded
- 1 cup shredded cheddar cheese + 1 tablespoon shredded cheddar cheese, divided
- 1 tbsp parmesan cheese, freshly grated
- 1 tsp dried parsley
- 1 tsp garlic powder
- Spray cooking oil

Preparation

- Preheat the oven to 350°F and grease a large baking dish.
- Spritz a baking sheet with cooking spray.
- Select a flat work surface and roll out your dough into a rectangle
- Brush 3 tablespoons of the melted butter on one side of the dough rectangle cornmeal and melted butter Cover the dough after flipping it over one side with mozzarella, Mexican cheese, and 1 cup of the sharp cheddar cheese
- Seal in the stuffing by folding the dough in half and pressing the edges together.
- Using your fingers, bring the dough's edges together.
- Spread the remaining melted butter over the dough

and set it aside sprinkle with the parmesan, the remaining cheddar cheese, and the basil. parsley, as well as onion and garlic powders

- To make it easier to roll out the dough, score it with 1-inch-deep lines.
- After baking, separate the ingredients.
- Bake the dough for 25 minutes at 350°F. Allow it to cool for 5 minutes before using. serving.

Chicken Pot Stickers from the Cheesecake Factory

This is a good recipe to make if you have guests coming over or if you just want to treat yourself. a small snack These chicken potstickers taste exactly like the ones served at the Cheesecake Factory a unique dish

Produces 48 – Time to Prepare: 15 minutes – Preparation Time: 45 minutes

Nutritional information per pot sticker: Calories: 75, Total Fat: 2 g, Carbohydrates: 18 g

4 g protein, 462 mg sodium

Ingredients

- Filling
- 1112 pound ground chicken
- 12 cup finely chopped red bell pepper
- 12 cup shredded green cabbage
- 13 cup finely chopped green onions
- 2 tsp ginger root, chopped
- 1 tbsp sesame oil
- 14 tsp white pepper
- Ingredients not listed
- 1 beaten egg white
- 1 cup of water
- 1 package round wonton skins (10 oz.)
- 4 cups chicken broth (distributed)
- divided 4 teaspoons reduced-sodium soy sauce
- Sauce pourable
- 1 cup chicken broth
- 14 tbsp soy sauce
- Garnish

- Finely sliced green onions or chive thin strips of nori (optional)

Preparation

- To make the filling, combine all of the filling ingredients in a mixing bowl.
- Using a fork, thoroughly incorporate each ingredient into the mixture.
- Wet the wonton skins one at a time.
- Spoon 1 tablespoon of the stuffing mixture into the center of the pie crust.
- Make 5 pleats on one side of the wrapper with wonton skin.
- Fold the wrapper over to seal in the mixture.
- Repeat steps 3 and 4 until you've used up all of your fillings.
- Grease a large skillet and cook pot stickers in batches on medium heat.
- Cook until they turn a light brown color. Avoid overcrowding the pan.
- Turn the heat up to medium-high. Pour 1 cup of the chicken broth into a mixing bowl and 1 teaspoon soy

sauce on top of the cooking pot stickers Cover

- Allow the mixture to sit in the pan until all of the liquid has evaporated.
- Place the potstickers on a plate and cover with foil to keep them warm.
- Steps 6 and 7 should be repeated for the remaining potstickers.
- Use the same pan to make the dipping sauce. 1 cup of chicken
- Bring broth and 14 cups soy sauce to a boil over high heat. Scrap the pan's bottom to extract all of the flavor Reduce the heat to
- Reduce the heat to medium and continue to cook

until the sauce has reduced by half, about 15 minutes.

- To serve, divide the potstickers among the serving plates and top with some of the
- Add the dipping sauce to the serving plate, then top with the potstickers.
- If desired, garnish with green onions or chives and thin strips of nori desired.

Cheddar Bay Biscuit from Red Lobster

You can make these biscuits in less than 40 minutes – and your guests will love them. Your family will be grateful!

9 servings – 15 minutes to prepare – Preparation Time: 25 minutes

Nutritional information per serving: Calories: 160, Total Fat: 10 g, Carbohydrates: 3 g

Sodium 380 mg, protein 16 g

Ingredients

- Biscuit:
- 2 dozen Bisquick biscuit mix
- 4 tbsp. chilled butter
- 1 cup grated sharp cheddar cheese

- 34 cup ice-cold whole milk
- 14 tsp garlic powder
- Glaze with Garlic Butter:
- 2 tablespoons melted butter
- 12 tsp garlic powder
- 14 tsp dried parsley flakes
- 1 tsp salt

Preparation

- Gather your materials by Preheat your oven to 450 degrees Fahrenheit; and Lightly grease a cookie sheet.
- Lightly combine the biscuit mix and the butter.
- •merged, but some small chunks remain
- Gently fold in the cheddar cheese, garlic powder, and milk.
- Once the ingredients have been evenly distributed, scoop 9 equal portions splatters of the mixture onto the cookie sheet
- Bake the biscuits for 15 to 17 minutes, or until the tops are light golden brown.

- While the biscuits are baking, make the glaze by combining all of the ingredients.
- In a small mixing bowl, combine the glaze ingredients.
- When the biscuits are done, place them on a cooling rack to cool.
- Before serving, brush the tops with the garlic butter glaze.

Buttermilk Biscuits from KFC

Here's another popular biscuit recipe. It only takes a little more than 20 minutes. It only takes a few minutes, but many people can attest to its delectability. 15 servings – 7 minutes to prepare – Preparation Time: 15 minutes Nutritional information per serving: Calories: 254.7, Total Fat: 13.1 g, Carbohydrates: 29.7 g 4.3 g protein, 659.3 mg sodium

Ingredients

- 12 cup melted butter
- 2 tbsp sugar + 112 tsp sugar, divided
- 1 beaten egg

- a quarter cup of buttermilk
- 14th Cup Club soda
- 1 teaspoon sea salt
- 5 c. Bisquick biscuit mix

Preparation

- Preheat the oven to 450 degrees Fahrenheit.
- Combine all of the ingredients to form a dough.
- Flour a flat surface, place the dough on it and roll it out. until it is a quarter-inch thick
- Cut the dough into pieces and shape them into biscuits.
- Arrange the cut dough on a baking sheet and bake for 12 to 15 minutes.

Enchiritos from Taco Bell

Simple but delectable If you're craving a sauce-covered taco, this recipe is for you is ideal for you. Serves 12 – Prep Time: 20 Minutes – Cook Time: 15 Minutes Calories 310, Total Fat 16 g, Carbohydrates 27 g, Protein 1 g 15 g protein, 1260 mg sodium

Ingredients

- Seasoning
- 14 cup unbleached all-purpose flour
- 1 teaspoon chili powder
- • 1 teaspoon sea salt
- 12 tsp dried onion flakes
- 12 tsp. paprika

- 14 tsp onion powder
- 1 teaspoon garlic powder
- Tortillas
- 1 pound ground beef, lean
- 12 cups of water
- 1 can (16 oz.) refried beans
- 12 flour tortillas, small
- 12 cup diced onion
- Red chili sauce, 116 oz.
- 2 cups shredded cheddar cheese
- For garnish, some green onions
- To serve, some sour cream

Preparation

- Combine all of the seasoning ingredients, then coat the beef.
- Using your hands, work the seasoning into the meat. Ensure that the beef is completely cooked. takes on the flavor of the spices
- Brown the seasoned beef in the water for 8 to 10 minutes over medium heat ten minutes Stir the

- beef occasionally to break up any lumps.
- While the beef is browning, microwave the beans for 2 minutes on high. Microwave the tortillas for 1 minute, wrapped in a wet towel.
- When the beef is finished, assemble the tortillas as follows:
- Arrange some beans in the center of the tortilla;
- Arrange some beef on top, followed by some onion;
- Roll the tortilla up by bringing the two ends together in the center;
- Place the tortilla in a microwave-safe dish; and
- Top the tortilla with chili sauce and cheddar cheese.
- Step 5 should be repeated until the casserole is full.
- Microwave the entire dish for 2-3 minutes on high. The dish is called
- When the cheese melts, the dish is finished.
- If desired, top with green onions and sour cream.

Spicy Queso Blanco from Applebee's

If you're going to serve chips at your next get-together, here's a dip to try This is the recipe that will make you famous among your guests. It tastes exactly like Applebee's!

1 14 cup – Preparation Time: 10 minutes – Cooking Time: 5 minutes Calories 1049, Total Fat 62 g, Carbohydrates 99 g, Protein 0 g 25 g protein, 2510 mg sodium

Ingredients

- Blanco Queso:
- 1 Tbsp. vegetable oil

- 12 minced small onion
- 1 to 3 jalapeno peppers, seeded, deveined, and minced
- 12 cup heavy cream
- 8 ounces Monterey Jack cheese, chunked
- 4 ounces chunked white American cheese
- 1 tablespoon chopped cilantro
- A little cooking oil
- Pico de Gallo:
- 12 small onion, diced
- 12 tablespoon chopped fresh cilantro
- 1 jalapeno, seeded, deveined, and minced
- 1 Roma tomato, seeded and diced

Preparation

- Sauté the onion and garlic in the oil over medium heat.
- 3 to 5 minutes, jalapenos
- Bring the heavy cream to a simmer in the mixture.
- Slowly add the cheese, stirring to ensure that all

- of the chunks melt. completely before adding any more
- When all of the cheese has melted, add the cilantro and mix well. When it comes to
- When the mixture is done, transfer it to a small bowl—this is your
- Queso Blanco.
- Make a simple Pico de Gallo by mixing all the Pico de Gallo
- Ingredients together in a medium-sized bowl.
- Top the Queso Blanco with some Pico de Gallo before serving.
-

Red Lobster's White Cheddar Mashed Potato

A mouthful of this creamy, cheesy mashed potato will have you asking for more. Bring the famous side dish from Red Lobster to your own home.

Serves 4 – Prep Time: 5 Minutes – Cook Time: 10 Minutes

Calories 490.7, Total Fat 31.4 g, Carbohydrates 41.4 g, Protein 1.4 g

12.7 g protein, 787.8 mg sodium

Ingredients

- 2 pounds peeled and quartered potatoes
- 2 oz. room temperature unsalted butter
- 13 cup heavy cream
- 14 cup soured cream
- 4 oz. grated white cheddar cheese
- 1 teaspoon sea salt
- 12 tsp white pepper

Preparation

- In a pot, bring some water to a boil, then add the potatoes inside.
- Continue to boil the potatoes until they are soft enough to mash. a knife
- Transfer the potatoes to a large mixing bowl once they are tender in a mixing bowl and mash them with a fork, potato masher, or electric mixer
- When there are no more chunks left, add the butter and continue to cook.
- Mash the potatoes until the butter is evenly distributed.

- Do the same with the heavy cream.
- Continue mixing after adding the sour cream.
- Slowly stir in the cheese, making sure it is thoroughly combined with the mashed potatoes.
- Serve the potatoes seasoned with salt and pepper.

Fried Green Beans from TGI Friday's

This nutritious snack is tasty as well as nutritious. Add a little crunch teat your meal in a healthy manner Serves 4 – Prep Time: 5 Minutes – Cook Time: 35 Minutes

Calories 441.2, Total Fat 20.8 g, Carbohydrates 52 g, Protein 1 g

11.7 g protein, 1093.5 mg sodium

Ingredients

- Beans, green:
- 4 cups broth (vegetable or chicken)
- fresh green beans, 6–8 oz.
- 1 beaten egg
- 1-quart milk

- 1 cup of flour
- 1 cup dry breadcrumbs, plain or seasoned
- a quarter teaspoon of salt
- 14 tsp onion powder
- 18 tsp garlic powder
- For frying, use vegetable oil or shortening.
- Dip: Wasabi Cucumber Ranch:
- 12 cup ranch dressing, bottled
- A 12 cup cucumber peeling, seeding, and chopping
- 1 Tbsp. milk
- 12 tsp prepared horseradish
- 1 tsp apple cider vinegar
- 1 tablespoon wasabi powder
- 18 teaspoon of salt
- 1 tsp cayenne pepper

Preparation

- Blend all of the dip ingredients in a blender. until completely smooth
- Refrigerate the mixture after placing it in a bowl.
- In a pot, bring the broth and green beans to a boil for 15 minutes.

- Take three shallow bowls for serving while the green beans are cooking.
- Dipping. In a separate bowl, whisk together the egg and milk. Place them in flour. In the third bowl, combine the breadcrumbs, salt, and onion. as well as garlic powder
- Remove the beans from the pot and place them in a bowl of cold water to cool.
- Transfer the beans to a dry bowl after shaking them dry.
- Dip the beans one at a time into the flour, then the egg mixture, and finally the oil breadcrumbs. Make certain that each bean is completely coated.
- In a pan, heat enough oil to cover the beans. Pour the oil over
- Preheat the oven to 350°F.
- Transfer the beans to a plate after they have turned golden brown wrapped in a paper towel
- When all of the beans are cooked, arrange them on a plate with the dip.
- Serve on a plate.

Hash Brown Casserole from Cracker Barrel

If the previous potato dish wasn't quite right for you, here's a hash. a brown recipe similar to Cracker barrels It's great for breakfast, lunch, and dinner or as a snack

Serves 10 – Prep Time: 15 Minutes – Cook Time: 45 Minutes

Calories 376.3, Total Fat 21.1 g, Carbohydrates 37.2 g, Protein 1.2 g Sodium 674.3 mg, 9.7 g protein

Ingredients

- 1 tbsp. melted butter or margarine
- 1-quart milk
- a 12 cup beef broth
- 1 tsp garlic salt (optional) or regular salt
- 14 tsp black pepper
- 14 cup minced or finely diced onions
- 26–30 ounces shredded hash browns
- 2 cups shredded cheddar cheese (distributed)

Preparation

- Preheat the oven to 425 degrees Fahrenheit and grease a 913 baking pan.
- In a mixing bowl, thoroughly combine the first 5 ingredients. Set aside.
- In a skillet, combine the hash browns and diced onions with half of the
- the layer of shredded cheese in the center Heat the skillet over medium heat.
- When the cheese begins to melt, begin folding the mixture.
- Place the heated hash browns in the baking pan and drizzle with the

the liquid mixture on top of them

- Combine the milk, broth, and hash browns in a mixing bowl until the hash browns are evenly coated.
- The liquid is absorbed by the hash browns.
- Smooth out the surface of the hash browns with a spatula spoon.
- Place in the oven, covered with foil. 30 minutes in the oven minutes.
- Remove the foil and top with the remaining cheese.
- Prepare to bake for another 10-15 minutes, or until the cheese has melted and turned golden brown.
- Allow cooling for 10 minutes before serving.

Onion Loaf by Tony Roma

Tony Roma serves onion rings as a loaf, which everyone enjoys. If you are

Here's how to make some at home.

Serves 6 – Prep Time: 30 Minutes – Cook Time: 15 Minutes

Calories 800, Total Fat 12 g, Carbohydrates 114 g, Protein 1 11 g protein, 1329 mg sodium

Ingredients

- 4–6 white onions
- 1-quart milk
- 3 beaten eggs
- Season with salt to taste
- 2 cups Bisquick/dry pancake mix
- Oil
- Garnish:
- Parsley

Preparation

- Cut the onions in half and remove the rings.
- In one bowl, combine the milk, eggs, and salt, and then place the
- In another, Bisquick.
- Allow the individual onion rings to soak in the egg mixture for thirty minutes
- Heat some oil when the onion rings are almost done soaking to 375°F
- 5. Cook the onion rings in the hot oil one at a time until they are golden brown.

- They're a golden brown color.
- While the onion rings are still hot, place them in an 84 loaf pan to pack them together—keep in mind: don't press; just let the oil do the work Its function.
- 7. Place the loaf on a plate after the onion rings have been set.
- Garnish with parsley.

Rosemary Bread from Romano's Macaroni Grill

Bread is an excellent snack. This aromatic loaf will raise your blood pressure. Whatever time of day you choose to consume it, it will be pumping. Serves 2 – Prep Time: 1 hour 10 minutes – Cook Time: 20 minutes

Calories 716.7, Total Fat 13.6 g, Carbohydrates 128.4 g, Protein 0.5 g

Sodium 1274.4 mg, 18.7 g protein

Ingredients

- a little olive oil
- 1 teaspoon instant yeast
- 1 teaspoon sugar

- 1 cup hot water
- 212 c. bread flour
- 1 teaspoon sea salt
- 1 tablespoon melted butter
- 2 tbsp rosemary (divided)

Preparation

- To begin, follow these steps:
    - Coat a bowl in olive oil;
    - Lightly grease a baking sheet or cookie sheet; and
    - Preheat the oven to 375 degrees Fahrenheit.
- In a food processor or mixing bowl, combine the yeast, sugar, and water.
- Allow resting.
- When the yeast mixture begins to bubble, add the remaining ingredients.
- Mix in all of the ingredients, reserving 1 tablespoon of rosemary for the end.
- Knead the dough by hand or in a food processor for 5 to 10 minutes.

- Place the dough in the refrigerator once it has become elastic and smooth.
- Cover the bowl with a towel after it has been greased. Allow the dough to rest for one hour
- When the dough has doubled in size, punch it down to flatten it. down. Then divide it in half.
- Set aside the two halves in separate bowls for now. Another ten minutes after allowing the dough to rest for 10 minutes, Form it into ovals.
- Top the dough with the remaining rosemary, pressing it in so that it is evenly distributed. becomes engrossed in the dough
- Allow the dough to rest for 45 minutes more.
- After the dough has rested for the final time, divide it into two halves.
- Place the pan in the oven and bake for 15 to 20 minutes.
- Remove the bread from the oven and set it aside to cool before slicing.
- Serving.

Chef John's Chicken Lettuce Wraps at P.F. Chang's

Here's P.F. if you're looking for a healthier snack. Chicken Chang's

Wraps made from lettuce It's filling and delicious!

Serves 8 – Prep Time: 35 Minutes – Cook Time: 15 Minutes

Calories 212, Total Fat 10.7 g, Carbohydrates 10.8 g, Protein 0.8 g

Sodium 332 mg, protein 17.6 g

Ingredients

- Chicken Combination:

- 112.25 pounds skinless, boneless chicken thighs, coarsely chopped
- 1 can (8 ounces) drained and minced water chestnuts
- 1 cup diced shiitake mushroom caps
- 12 cup minced yellow onion
- 13 cup chopped green onion
- 1 teaspoon soy sauce
- 1 tbsp. freshly grated ginger
- 2 tablespoons brown sugar
- two tbsp vegetable oil
- Glaze:
- 14 cup chicken broth
- 14 cup risotto wine vinegar
- 4 minced garlic cloves
- 1 tbsp. ketchup
- 1 teaspoon soy sauce
- 2 tbsp. sesame oil
- 2 tablespoons brown sugar
- 12 tsp red pepper flakes

- 12 tsp dry mustard
- Wrap and herbs:
- 12 tbsp fresh cilantro, chopped
- 12 tbsp. fresh basil, chopped
- 12 tablespoons chopped green onion
- 16 iceberg lettuce leaves, or as needed

Preparation

- In a mixing bowl, combine all of the chicken mix ingredients (except the oil) bowl
- . Wrap the bowl in plastic wrap and place it in the refrigerator.
- Whisk together all of the glaze ingredients until well combined thoroughly.
- When the glaze is finished, cook the chicken mixture ingredients in the
- Heat the oil over high heat.
- When the chicken has been cooked for 2 minutes, pour half of the
- Pour the glaze over the chicken mixture. Cook the entire mixture for another 5 minutes until the glaze

begins to caramelize this should take between 10 and 15 minutes.

- Reduce the heat to medium-low and stir in the remaining glaze. to the combination Cook for another 3 minutes, stirring constantly stirring.
- Add the chopped herbs (cilantro, basil, and onion) and mix well Cook until they are fully incorporated into the chicken. mixture.
- Place the chicken on a plate and top with lettuce.
- Soup Recipes That Aren't Yours

French Onion Soup from Outback

This decadent French onion soup is simple to make and can serve as a meal on its own on its own If you enjoy Outback's signature dishes, here's one to try which you can prepare for dinner

Serves 4 – Prep Time: 15 Minutes – Cook Time: 50 Minutes

Calories 420, Total Fat 29 g, Carbohydrates 21 g, Protein 1 g

19 g protein, 2120 mg sodium

Ingredients:

- 2 cups quartered and sliced sweet yellow onion
- 12 cup sweetened cream butter

- 12 teaspoon of salt
- 1 Tbsp. flour
- 4 cups beef broth
- 1 tablespoon thyme, fresh
- 1 teaspoon black pepper, coarsely ground
- 4 baguette slices, about 12 inches thick
- Provolone cheese, 8 slices

Directions:

- In a medium-sized stockpot, melt the butter.

• Sauté the onions and salt for 3 minutes, or until softened. However, it is not browned. Add the flour and stir to combine. Bring the beef stock to a boil over medium-high heat. Bring to a boil Allow to boil for 1 minute. Reduce to low heat and season with thyme and black pepper.

- Allow simmering for 25-30 minutes, covered.

While the soup is cooking, toast the baguette slices to a crisp. Golden brown. Check that each slice fits comfortably in the soup bowl Preheat the oven to broil. When the soup has finished simmering, ladle it into oven-safe bowls. bowls for serving Each bowl should be topped with a toasted baguette slice and two slices of

- The cheese is provolone. Broil for 1-2 minutes, or until golden brown until the cheese has melted and begun to caramelize
- Carefully remove from the broiler and serve immediately.

Black Bean Soup from T.G.I. Friday's

This soup is ideal for a cold, rainy day. If you're in the mood for T.G.I. Friday's, this is the place to be. If you missed out on Friday's black bean soup, here's a recipe you can make right now Serves 6 – Prep Time: 10 Minutes – Cook Time: 1 Hour 15 Minutes

Calories 392.5, Total Fat 7.8 g, Carbohydrates 59.3 g, Protein 0.5 g Sodium 458.9 mg, protein 23 g

Ingredients

- two tbsp vegetable oil
- 14 cup diced white onion

- 12 cup diced carrot
- 14 cup diced green bell pepper
- 2 tablespoons minced garlic
- 4 rinsed 15-ounce cans of black beans
- 4 cup chicken broth
- 2 tbsp. apple cider vinegar
- 2 tablespoons chili powder
- 12 tsp cayenne pepper
- a quarter teaspoon cumin
- 12 teaspoon of salt
- 14 teaspoon liquid hickory smoke

Preparation

- Sauté the onion, celery, carrot, bell pepper, and garlic in a pan in olive oil. 15 minutes on low heat in the heated oil Keep in mind to preventing the vegetables from burning
- While the vegetables cook, strain and wash the black beans.

- In a large pot, combine 3 cups of washed beans and 1 cup chicken stock.
- Purée in a food processor until smooth.
- When the onion mixture is done, add the remaining ingredients. (along with the bean purée) to the pan.
- Bring everything to a boil, then reduce the heat and let it sit for a few minutes.
- Allow the mixture to simmer for an additional 50 to 60 minutes.
- Serve the soup in individual bowls.

Minestrone Soup from Olive Garden

Minestrone is a traditional Italian dish. Here's Olive Garden's take on this well-known dish. Serves 8 – Prep Time: 5 Minutes – Cook Time: 40 Minutes Calories 353.5, Total Fat 6.3 g, Carbohydrates 57.8 g, Protein 0.5 g

Sodium 471.7 mg, 19.2 g protein

Ingredients

- three tbsp olive oil
- 12 cup sliced green beans
- 14 cup diced celery

- 1 cup diced white onion
- 1 diced zucchini
- 4 tbsp. minced garlic
- 4 cups veggie broth
- 1 can (15 oz.) red kidney beans, drained
- 2 cans (15 oz.) small white beans, drained
- 1 can (14 oz.) diced tomatoes
- 1 peeled and diced carrot
- 2 tbsp finely chopped fresh Italian parsley
- 12 tsp dried oregano
- 12 teaspoons of salt
- 12 tsp ground black pepper
- 12 tsp dried basil
- 14 tsp dried thyme
- 3 cups boiling water
- 4 cups baby spinach, fresh
- 12 cup tiny shell pasta
- Parmesan cheese, shredded, for serving
- Preparation
- Chop and mince the ingredients according to package directions. In olive oil, sauté the green beans, celery, onion, zucchini, and garlic.

- In a soup pot, heat the oil until the onions are translucent.
- Except for the beans, pasta, and cheese, combine the remaining ingredients in a mixing bowl.
- Bring the spinach leaves and water to a boil in a saucepan.
- When the mixture reaches a boil, add the beans, spinach, and pasta.
- Reduce the heat to low and continue to cook for another 20 minutes.
- Ladle into a bowl, top with parmesan cheese, and serve.

Vegetarian Summer Corn Chowder from Panera Bread

On a cold, rainy night, pair some bread with this delicious soup for dinner. night. It's cozy and warm. Serves 6 – Prep Time: 10 Minutes – Cook Time: 45 Minutes Calories 320, Total Fat 20 g, Carbohydrates 34 g, Protein 1 g

5 g protein, 1310 mg sodium

Ingredients

- 2 teaspoons olive oil
- 1 tbsp. unsalted butter
- 1 medium diced red onion

- 3 tbsp. all-purpose flour
- 2 diced russet potatoes
- 5 cups vegetable stock, unsalted
- 12 cup diced red bell pepper
- 12 cup diced green bell pepper
- 4 cups whole kernel corn
- 14 teaspoon ground black pepper
- 1 cup cream (half-and-half)
- Season with salt and pepper to taste.
- Thinly sliced chives for garnish
- Bacon bits as a garnish

Preparation

- Over low heat, sauté the onion in butter and oil. When the onion is sliced
- When the onion is translucent, add the flour and cook for another 5 minutes. minutes.
- Add the potatoes, diced into quarter-inch cubes, to the mixture is simmering.

Turn up the heat and add the broth.

- Bring the mixture to a rolling boil.
- Reduce the heat to medium and continue to cook for 15 minutes
- .Add the bell peppers, diced into quarter-inch cubes, to the mixture. Add the corn, pepper, cream, salt, and pepper to taste.
- Allow the mixture to simmer for an additional 15 minutes. Place the soup in a bowl and top with chives and bacon if so desired

Clam Chowder from Red Lobster

This recipe perfectly recreates Red Lobster's seafood chowder soup. Have fun with this. When you're in the mood for a creamy soup, make it. Serves 8 – Prep Time: 20 Minutes – Cook Time: 30 Minutes Calories 436.1, Total Fat 26.5 g, Carbohydrates 30.1 g, Protein 0.1 g

20.3 g protein, 1987 mg sodium

Ingredients

2 tablespoons melted butter

- 1 cup diced onion
- 12 cup thinly sliced white part of a leek
- 14 teaspoon minced garlic

- two tbsp flour
- 4 quarts milk
- 1 cup diced clams with juice
- 1 cup diced potato
- 1 teaspoon salt
- 14 tsp white pepper
- 1 tsp. dried thyme
- 12 cup heavy cream
- For serving, use saltine crackers.

Preparation

- Sauté the onion, leek, garlic, and celery in butter in a pot over medium heat.
- Remove the vegetables from the heat after 3 minutes and add the flour.
- Incorporate the milk and clam juice.
- Bring the mixture back to a boil by returning it to heat.
- Reduce the heat to low and add potatoes, salt, pepper, and thyme.

- Allow the mixture to simmer. Mix for an additional 10 minutes. while the soup is cooking
- Allow the mixture to simmer for 5 to 8 minutes after adding the clams. or until the clams are tender.
- Cook for a few minutes more after adding the heavy cream.
- Transfer the soup to a bowl and top with saltine crackers to serve.

Mama Mandola Sicilian Chicken Soup from Carrabba's

Have you ever eaten Carrabba's chicken soup? It's a fantastic combination of heartiness and sweetness and a creaminess that will take your taste buds to the heavens.

Serves 10 – Prep Time: 15 Minutes – Cook Time: 8 Hours Calories 320, Total Fat 0 g, Carbohydrates 57 g, Protein 1 g 13 g protein, 525.3 mg sodium

Ingredients

- 4 peeled and diced carrots
- 4 celery stalks, diced
- 1 green bell pepper, peeled and diced

- 2 medium diced white potatoes
- 1 diced white onion
- 3 minced garlic cloves
- 1 can (14.5 oz.) diced tomatoes with juice
- 1 tablespoon parsley, fresh
- 1 tsp Italian seasoning
- 12 tsp white pepper
- To taste, a dash of crushed red pepper flakes
- 2 shredded boneless skinless chicken breasts
- 2 cans (32 oz.) chicken stock
- 1/12 teaspoon salt
- 1 pound fettuccine ditalini

Preparation

- As directed, dice and chop the vegetables.
- Put them in a slow cooker and top them with parsley. seasoning, as well as white and red pepper Combine all of the ingredients.
- Mix in the shredded chicken and stock once more.

- Cook the mixture, covered, for 8 hours on low heat.
- When the soup is nearly done, bring a salt-and-water mixture to a boil. a boil to cook the pasta
- Cook for 5 minutes after adding the cooked pasta to the soup. minutes, then serve.

Soup with Sausage and Lentils by arrabba

If you like Carrabba's soups, here's another one for you. Bring Carrabba's with you. bring your family's favourite sausage and lentil soup to the table. Serves 6 – Prep Time: 10 Minutes – Cook Time: 1 Hour 5 Minutes

Calories 221, Total Fat 10 g, Carbohydrates 20 g, Protein 1 g

13 g protein, 1182 mg sodium

Ingredients

- Italian sausages weighing 1 pound
- 1 large diced onion

- 1 celery stalk, diced
- 2 large diced carrots
- 1 small diced zucchini
- 6 cups chicken broth (low sodium)
- 2 cans (14.5 oz. each) diced tomatoes with juice
- 2 cup dried lentils
- 2–3 minced garlic cloves
- 1/12 teaspoon salt
- 1 teaspoon ground black pepper
- 1-3 pinches red pepper flakes (or more if you like it hotter)
- 1 tsp dried basil
- 12 tsp dried oregano
- 12 tsp. parsley
- 12 teaspoon dried thyme
- Garnish with parmesan cheese

Preparation

- Preheat the oven to 350 degrees Fahrenheit. Place the sausages in a baking dish and bake for 20 minutes.
- Using a fork, make a few holes in each sausage. Bake for 20-30 minutes or until the sausages are cooked through. Allow to cool before slicing the sauerkraut
- Chop and mince the ingredients as directed on the package list.
- In a large mixing bowl, combine all of the ingredients except the parmesan cheese.pot..
- Bring the soup to a boil, then reduce to a low heat and cover.
- Allow the mixture to simmer for an hour, adding water as needed to reduce. when needed, thickness Puree a potato if you want a thicker soup. return a portion of the soup
- Pour the soup into bowls and top with parmesan cheese. prior to serving

Denny's Beef and Vegetable Barley Soup

If you're looking for a beefy, rich soup, this is the one for you. desires This dish is sure to whet your appetite.

4 servings – 10 minutes to prepare – 40 minutes to cook

Calories 244.5, Total Fat 11.4 g, Carbs 17.1 g, Protein 0.5

20 g protein, 1818.2 mg sodium

Ingredients

- 12 lb. ground beef
- Frozen mixed vegetables, 16 oz.
- 1 can (14.5 oz.) diced tomatoes with juice
- 32 oz. beef broth

- seasoned with salt and pepper

Preparation

- Cook the ground beef in a pot until it is brown.
- Bring the vegetables, tomatoes, barley, and broth to a boil.
- Bring the entire mixture to a boil.
- Season with salt and pepper and set aside to cool.
- Allow at least 40 minutes to simmer.
- Ladle the soup into individual bowls and serve. The longer you stay, the more
- The longer you leave the soup to simmer, the better it will taste.

Walkabout Soup from Outback

Don't pass up this creamy delight just because you don't want to. Get out of the house. Here's a recipe that tastes exactly like Outback's signature soup.

Serves 4 – Prep Time: 10 Minutes – Cook Time: 45 Minutes Calories 329, Total Fat 25 g, Carbohydrates 17 g, Protein 1 g 6 g protein, 1061 mg sodium

Ingredients

- Sauce: Thick white sauce:
- 3 tablespoons melted butter
- three tbsp flour

- 14 teaspoon of salt
- 1 12 cup whole milk
- Soup:
- 2 cups thinly sliced yellow sweet onions
- 3 tablespoons melted butter
- 1 tin (14.5 oz.) chicken broth
- 12 teaspoon of salt
- 14 tsp freshly ground black pepper
- 2 cubes chicken bouillon
- 14 cup diced Velveeta cubes, packed
- 112–134 cup white sauce (recipe above)
- Shredded Cheddar cheese for garnish
- For serving, use crusty bread.

Preparation

- First, make the thick white sauce. Cook melted butter to make a roux. Melt the butter and flour together over medium heat. Pour the milk slowly onto the roux, a little at a time, while stirring constantly.
- Remove the mixture when it has reached a pudding-like consistency.

- Remove from heat and set aside.
  - Sauté the onions in the butter in a soup pot over medium heat. until they turn translucent
  - Except for the cheese and white wine, combine the remaining ingredients in a mixing bowl.
  - Add the sauce to the pot and combine everything.
  - When the mixture is completely heated, add the cheese and sauce blanche Bring the entire mixture to a medium-low boil. heat.
- Continue to stir the soup until everything is combined. completely blended together
- When the cheese has melted, reduce the heat and continue to cook.
- Cook the soup for an additional 30 to 45 minutes.
- Pour the soup into bowls and top with cheese. Pair with a slice of bread

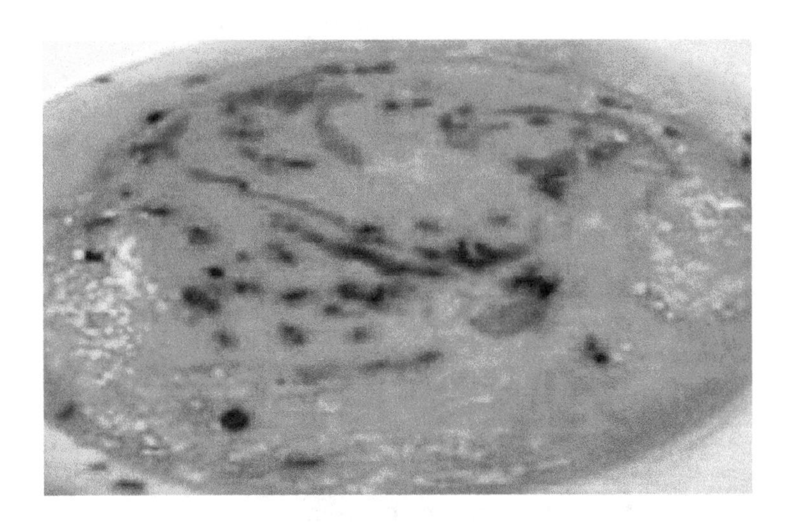

Soup with Butternut Squash from Wolfgang Puck

Creamy squash soup is always a hit. This butternut squash soup is delicious. The ideal appetizer you've been searching for. 2 quarts – Preparation Time: 25 minutes – Cooking Time: 1 hour 20 minutes

Calories 1293.8 per batch, Total Fat 64.3 g, Carbohydrates 172.8 g Sodium 1296.3 mg, protein 27.9 g

Ingredients

- Soup:
- 334 pounds of butternut squash
- Acorn squash (134 pounds)

- 6 tbsp unsalted butter (divided)
- 1 finely diced onion
- 12 tsp kosher salt
- 18 tsp fresh white pepper
- 14 tsp ground nutmeg
- 14 teaspoon ground ginger
- 18 teaspoon cardamom powder
- 4 cups warmed chicken or vegetable stock
- 12 c. crème fraiche
- 1 tablespoon fresh chives, thinly sliced
- Coulis of Roasted Red Peppers
- 2 roasted red bell peppers
- 14 cup broth (chicken)
- seasoned with salt and pepper

Preparation

- Preheat the oven to 350 degrees Fahrenheit. 2 tablespoons of butter, melted
- Season with salt, pepper, and nutmeg, to taste.

- Cut the squashes in half, remove the seeds, and set aside.as well as brushing the cut sides with seasoned butter
- Arrange the squashes cut-side down on a baking sheet. Bake for an hour.
- When the squashes are soft, scoop them into a bowl and season with salt and pepper. purée. Set aside the squash purée.
- Over low heat, sauté the onions in 4 tablespoons butter. Not at all.
- Allow them to brown.
- When the onions have turned translucent, add the squash purée.
- Allow the mixture to continue to cook. Make certain that the
- There is no simmering or boiling in the mixture.
- When the mixture is thoroughly heated, add the ginger and cardamom, followed by the stock

- Bring the mixture to a boil without increasing the heat. Allow
- Allow the mixture to simmer for 20 minutes, stirring occasionally.
- In the meantime, make the red pepper coulis:
- Roast the bell peppers over high heat until the skin is charred, about 15 minutes. reheat the oven to broil. Allow the pepper to cool.
- Remove the skins from the peppers and purée the flesh in a food processor.
- Pour in the chicken broth slowly.
- Season with salt and pepper to taste.
- Pour into a sauce bottle and set aside.
- When the mixture has finished cooking, stir in the crème fraiche. as well as chives
- When the flavours have blended, remove the rosemary sprig and set aside. Season the soup to taste. Pour the mixture into a bowl and top with the red pepper coulis before serving, make swirls in the soup

The Monterey Clam Chowder at Disneyland

Make a magical dish from the most magical place on the planet. This clam is Chowder soup will undoubtedly take your taste buds on a wild ride. Serves 4 – Prep Time: 15 Minutes – Cook Time: 1 Hour

Calories 472.3, Total Fat 36.9 g, Carbohydrates 27.4 g, Protein 2.4 g Sodium 771.5 mg, 9.3 g protein

Ingredients

- 5 tablespoons melted butter
- flour 5 tbsp

- two tbsp vegetable oil
- 1 12 cup potatoes (peeled, diced)
- 12 cup diced onion
- 12 cup crushed red pepper
- 12 cup fresh green pepper
- a 12 cup celery
- 2 14 cup clam juice
- 12 quarts heavy cream
- 1 cup chopped clams
- 1 tbsp. fresh thyme or 12 tbsp. dried thyme
- 14–12 teaspoon salt
- 1 tsp white pepper
- 13–12 tsp Tabasco sauce
- 4 sourdoughs round bread bowls made from individual sourdough round breads
- Garnish with chives (optional)

Preparation

- Over medium heat, make a roux by combining melted butter and flour. for ten minutes

- Flour burns quickly, so keep an eye on it.
- Mix everything together thoroughly. Set aside the roux. For 10 minutes, sauté the potatoes, onions, peppers, and celery in the oil.
- Using a soup pot, cook for 30 minutes.
- Whisk in the remaining ingredients, including the roux.
- Bring the entire mixture to a boil in a soup pot.
- After the mixture has boiled, reduce the heat and allow it to simmer for a few minutes.
- Season the soup with salt and pepper to taste. To serve, use a ladle.
- Distribute the soup evenly among the prepared bread bowls and top with
- If desired, garnish with fresh chives.
- Chicken Recipes That Aren't Yours

Chicken from Chipotle

This dish is sure to be a hit at your next gathering. Or perhaps a family dinner. Or whatever you want! It's simple but delicious.

Serves 8 – Preparation. Time: 10 minutes – Marinate Time: 24 hours – Cook Time: 20 minutes

Calories 293, Total Fat 18.7 g, Carbohydrates 5.8 g, Protein 0.5 g Sodium 526 mg, protein 24.9 g

Ingredients

- 2 12 pound boneless and skinless organic boneless and skinless chicken breasts or thighs Cooking spray or olive oil

- Marinade
- 7.5 oz. Adobo-spiced chipotle peppers
- 2 teaspoons olive oil
- 6 peeled garlic cloves
- 1 teaspoon ground black pepper
- a teaspoon of salt
- a quarter teaspoon cumin
- 12 tsp dried oregano

Preparation

- In a food processor or blender, combine all of the marinade ingredients.
- and blend until a smooth paste is formed.
- Pound the chicken until it is between 12 and 34 inches thick.
- Put the chicken in an airtight container or a resalable plastic bag.
- a Ziploc bag, for example Pour the marinade over the chicken and toss to coat.

until thoroughly coated Place the chicken in the refrigerator and allow it to chill. marinate for at least 12 hours and up to 24 hours.

- Pour the blended mixture into the container and marinate it for 30 minutes.
- For at least 8 hours, marinate the chicken.
- Cook the chicken in an oiled skillet over medium-high heat.
- Grill for 3 to 5 minutes per side on a preheated grill. The internal structure
- Before you remove the chicken, it should be 165 degrees Fahrenheit. due to the heat It can also be cooked in a heavy-bottomed skillet.
- with a little olive oil over medium heat
- Allow to rest before serving. Cut into cubes to add to salads if desired.
- tacos or quesadillas, or simply serve as is

Popeye's Fried Chicken

Fried chicken is a popular dish among children. If your kids love Popeye's If you want to make your own version, here's a recipe you can make in your own kitchen.

Serves: 8 – Preparation Time: 20 minutes – Cooking Time: 45 minutes

Calories 733, Total Fat 26.8 g, Carbohydrates 76.3 g, Protein 0.7 g

Protein 44.3 g, Sodium 3140 mg

Ingredients

- Breading:
- 3 cups self-rising flour
- 1 cup corn starch
- 3 tablespoons seasoning salt
- 2 tablespoons paprika
- 1 teaspoon baking soda
- 1 package (0.7 ounce) dry Italian-style salad dressing mix
- 1 package (1 ounce) dry onion soup mix
- 1 (1 ½ ounces) packet dry spaghetti sauce spices and seasoning mix
- 3 tablespoons white sugar
- Batter/Coating:
- 3 cups cornflakes cereal, crushed
- 2 eggs, beaten
- ¼ cup cold water
- Chicken:
- 2 cups oil for frying

- 1 (4-pound) whole chicken, cut into pieces

Preparation

- Mix all of the breading ingredients together in a deep bowl.
- Place the crushed cereal in another bowl.
- In another bowl, beat the eggs and cold water together.
- Heat the oil to 350°F and preheat the oven to 350°F.
- Dip the chicken into the breading mixture, the egg mixture, the
- Crushed cereal, and then the breading mixture again.
- Immediately place the breaded chicken into the heated oil and
- Cook on each side for 3 to 4 minutes.
- Place the chicken in a 9×13 baking pan skin-side up. Cover the
- Baking pan with foil, leaving a small opening.

- Bake the chicken for 45 minutes.
- After 45 minutes, remove the foil and continue baking for
- 5 minutes more.
- Remove the baking pan from the oven and serve.

McDonald's Chicken Nuggets

Chicken nuggets are tasty, but kind of unhealthy. This all-natural recipe will give you a healthy alternative to the McDonald's version.

Serves: 4 – Preparation Time: 1 hour 45 minutes – Cooking Time: 45 minutes

Nutrition facts per serving: Calories 370.5, Total Fat 5 g, Carbs 44.9 g,

Protein 33.2 g, Sodium 1457.4 mg

Ingredients

- Chicken:
- 1 pound chicken tenderloins, boneless and thawed
- Brine:
- 4 cups water, cold
- 2 teaspoons fine sea salt
- Breading:
- ⅓ + ½ cup all-purpose flour, sifted
- All-purpose flour, sifted
- ½ cup corn starch
- 1½ tablespoons seasoned salt
- 1 tablespoon fine corn flour
- 1½ teaspoons dry milk powder, non-fat
- 1 teaspoon granulated sugar
- ½ teaspoon ginger, ground
- ¼ teaspoon mustard, ground
- ¼ teaspoon black pepper, fine

- ¼ teaspoon white pepper, fine
- ⅛ teaspoon allspice, ground
- ⅛ teaspoon cloves, ground
- ⅛ teaspoon paprika, ground
- ⅛ teaspoon turmeric, ground
- 1 pinch cinnamon, ground
- 1 pinch cayenne pepper
- Batter:
- 2 eggs, beaten
- ½ cup water, cold
- 2 tablespoons corn starch
- 2 tablespoons all-purpose flour
- ¼ teaspoon sea salt, fine
- ¼ teaspoon sesame oil
- ¼ teaspoon soy sauce
- ¼ teaspoon granulated sugar
- For Deep Frying:
- Vegetable oil, 3 parts
- Vegetable shortening, 1 part

Preparation

- Pound the chicken until it is only ½ inch thick.
- Mix the brine ingredients.
- Cut the chicken into small, chicken-nugget-sized pieces and
- place them in the brine. Leave it in the refrigerator for 2 hours.
- When the chicken is almost done soaking,

  whisk together all the batter ingredients. Also mix together all the breading ingredients.
- Remove the chicken from the refrigerator and evenly coat each piece with the batter.
- Evenly coat each battered piece with the breading.
- Slowly heat the deep-frying ingredients to 350°F.
- Deep fry each nugget and then transfer to a plate with a paper towel to drain the oil.

- Transfer to a different plate and serve.

Note: The nuggets can be battered up and breaded in advance and stored in an airtight container if you want to fry them later

Sonora Chicken Pasta from Ruby Tuesday

Pasta is both filling and tasty. Here's a quick meal you can make. whenever you're in the mood for some comfort food

Serves 4 – Prep Time: 25 Minutes – Cook Time: 20 Minutes

Calories 966, Total Fat 18 g, Carbohydrates 34 g, Protein 1 gSodium 0 mg, Protein 0 g

Ingredients

- Mixture of Cheeses
- 1 pound Velveeta-style processed cheese
- 12 cup heavy cream
- 2 tablespoons olive oil
- 2 tbsp. minced red chili peppers
- 2 tbsp. minced green chili peppers
- 2 tablespoons minced onions
- 12 minced garlic clove
- 2 teaspoons water
- 14 teaspoon of salt
- 2 tablespoons sugar
- 12 teaspoon vinegar
- a quarter teaspoon cumin
- Beans
- 1 can (15 oz.) black beans, with water
- 2 tbsp. minced green chili peppers
- 2 tablespoons minced onions
- 12 minced garlic clove

- 14 teaspoon of salt1 tsp paprika
- Chicken and seasoning:
- Oil from vegetables
- 12 teaspoon of salt
- 1 teaspoon dried thyme
- 1 tablespoon dried summer savory
- 4 boneless, skinless chicken breast halves
- Pasta:
- 1 penne pasta box (16 oz.)
- four quarts of water
- 1 tablespoon melted butter
- Garnish:
- chopped green onion
- Diced tomatoes

Preparation

- Preheat the grill.
- Over low heat, combine the Velveeta and cream until smooth.

- In a separate pan, heat the olive oil and sauté the peppers, onions, and garlic.and a clove of garlic
- After 2 minutes, add the water and return to a simmer for another 2 minutes.
- Continue to simmer the cheese with the sautéed vegetables. on low heat Mix in the salt, sugar, vinegar, and the cumin, and cook the whole thing on low heat. Make certain to stir.
- In a separate saucepan, combine the beans, peppers, onions, garlic, salt, and pepper.
- Bring the water, paprika, and salt to a boil over medium heat.
- Reduce the heat to low once the bean mixture begins to boil. Keep it on the stove.
- Combine all of the seasoning ingredients and rub the seasoning all over the meat. atop the chicken
- Cook the chicken in oil for 5 minutes on each side. and then cut the chicken into 12-inch slices

- Bring the pasta to a boil in the water. When the pasta is done, drain it and set it aside.
- While the noodles are still hot, mix in the butter.
- Assemble the dish by smothering the pasta in sauce and arranging the vegetables on top.
- After that, pour the bean mixture over it, followed by the chicken. Finish with a garnish. dish by sprinkling the tomatoes and green onions on top.

Parmesan Crusted Chicken from Olive Garden

This pasta has a crunchy twist that pleases the palate. You can also make it in less than an hour!

Serves 4 – Prep Time: 15 Minutes – Cook Time: 40 Minutes Calories 1231, Total Fat 60.4 g, Carbohydrates 128.7 g, Protein 0.7 g 33.4 g protein, 1406.1 mg sodium

Ingredients

- Breading:
- 1 cup unseasoned breadcrumbs
- two tbsp flour
- 14 cup parmesan cheese, grated

- To dip in:
- 1-quart milk
- Chicken:
- 2 breasts of chicken
- Frying oil made from vegetables
- 2 cups linguini pasta, cooked
- 2 tablespoons melted butter
- three tbsp olive oil
- 2 tsp. crushed garlic
- 12 oz. white wine
- 14 cups of water
- two tbsp flour
- a quarter cup half-and-half
- 14 cup soured cream
- 12 teaspoon of salt
- 1 teaspoon finely diced fresh flat-leaf parsley34 cup mild Asiago cheese grated finely
- Garnish:

- 1 diced Roma tomato
- Parmesan cheese, grated
- Finely chopped fresh flat-leaf parsley

Preparation

- Pound the chicken until it is 12 inches thick.
- Place the breading ingredients in a shallow bowl and set them aside.
- milk in a different container
- Heat some oil in a skillet over medium to medium-low heat.
- Dip the chicken in the breading, then in the milk, and finally in the breading. again. Place immediately in hot oil.
- Cook the chicken in the oil for 3-4 minutes, or until golden brown.
- 1 minute per side Remove the chicken and place it on a plate. A liner of paper towels
- Make a roux by whisking flour into heated olive oil and butter.
- Heat to medium.

- When the roux has finished cooking, add the garlic, water, and salt to the pan and toss
- Continue stirring and cooking after adding the wine.
- Stir in the half-and-half and sour cream until well combined.
- Allow the cheese to melt.
- Finally, remove from the heat and stir in the parsley. Mix in the pasta
- To coat, stir everything together.
- Distribute the hot pasta among the serving plates.
- Sprinkle the chicken, diced tomatoes, and parmesan cheese on top of each dish.
- Before serving, add the cheese.

Chicken Marsala from Olive Garden

A traditional favorite from one of America's favorite Italian restaurants. So simple to make and so delicious.

Serves 4-6 people – Prep Time: 10 minutes – Cook Time: 40 minutes

Calories 950, Total Fat 58 g, Carbohydrates 71 g, Protein 1 g 66 g protein, 1910 mg sodium

Ingredients

- 2 teaspoons olive oil
- 2 tablespoons melted butter

- 4 skinless boneless chicken breasts
- 12 cup thinly sliced mushrooms
- 1 garlic clove, thinly sliced
- For dredging, use flour.
- Black pepper, freshly ground, and sea salt
- 12 cup chicken broth
- 1 tbsp Marsala wine
- 1 teaspoon lemon juice
- 1 tablespoon Dijon mustard

Preparation

- Spaghetti with chicken scaloppini
- Using a mallet or rolling pin, pound the chicken to about 12 oz.one-inch thick
- Heat the olive oil and 1 tablespoon of the butter in a large skillet.
- over a medium-high flame Dredge the chicken in the flour when the oil is hot.

  in the flour Season both sides with salt and pepper. Only dredge as many as you can fit in the skillet Avoid overcrowding the pan.

- Cook the chicken in batches for 1 to 2 minutes on each side or until done until
- thoroughly cooked Remove from skillet and place on an oven-safe plate.
- While the rest of the chicken is cooking, keep it warm in the oven cooked.
- 1 tablespoon olive oil in the same skillet set to medium-high
- Sauté mushrooms and garlic until softened in a skillet over medium heat. Remove the mushrooms from the pan and set them aside.
- Add the chicken stock and scrape up any stray bits in the pan.
- Reduce by half on high heat, about 6-8 minutes. Marsala should be added. reduce by half the amount of wine and lemon juice approximately 6–8 minutes Return the mushroom to the saucepan, and

Add the Dijon mustard and mix well. 1 minute on medium-low heat heat. Remove from the heat and stir in the remaining butter to make the sauce smoother sauce

- Pour the sauce over the chicken and serve immediately.

Crispy Honey-Chipotle Chicken Crispers from Chili's

Fried chicken is sometimes the only option. Make this easy recipe at You'll be glad you did when you get home because your family and stomach will thank you.

Serves 4 – Prep Time: 15 Minutes – Cook Time: 30 Minutes

Calories 492 per serving, Total Fat 3.3 g, Carbohydrates 107.2 g 11.2 g protein, 2331.5 mg sodium

Ingredients

- tenderloins of chicken
- 6 cups vegetable oil or shortening for frying
- Honey-Chipotle Relish:
- 2/3 cup honey
- 14 cups of water
- 14 cups of ketchup
- 1 Tbsp. white vinegar
- 2 teaspoons ground or powdered chipotle chili pepper
- 12 teaspoon of salt
- Batter:
- 1 beaten egg
- 12 cup unsweetened condensed milk
- 12 cup chicken broth (approximately)
- 12 teaspoons of salt
- 14 tsp black pepper
- 14 tsp. paprika
- 14 tsp garlic powder

a quarter cup all-purpose flour

- Breading:
- 1 12 cups all-purpose flour
- 12 teaspoons of salt
- a quarter teaspoon paprika
- 12 tsp black pepper
- 12 tsp garlic powder
- Garnish
- Fries à la française
- The corn on the cob
- Ranch dressing for dipping

Preparation

- In a saucepan, combine all of the chipotle sauce ingredients and heat through.
- Bring the water to a boil over medium heat. When the sauce begins to boil,
- Reduce to a simmer for another two minutes before serving removing from the heat
- Preheat the oil to 350 degrees Fahrenheit. While you're waiting for your oil to heat up,

- While the batter is heating, whisk together all of the ingredients (except the flour).

  for 30 seconds, or until completely combined When everything is in order

- After you've mixed everything, add the flour and mix it all together again.

  In a separate bowl, combine all of the breading ingredients.

- Place the batter and breading bowls next to each other to form a triangle your painting station The oil should be hot enough at this point.

- Dip the chicken into the batter, allowing excess batter to drip off, and serve. Then coat it in the breading.

- Place the breaded chicken on a plate and begin frying two pieces at a time the maximum amount of time Allows each chicken piece to sit in the oil for at least 4 minutes.

- Cover a plate with paper towels to prepare

- When the chicken is done cooking, transfer it to a plate lined with paper towels to allow the oil to drain
- Allow the fried chicken to cool before transferring it to a large bowl.
- Toss everything together with the sauce. Make certain that you
- Cover the chicken with the sauce.
- Transfer to a plate and serve with French fries and corn on the cob the cub, as well as a ranch dipping sauce

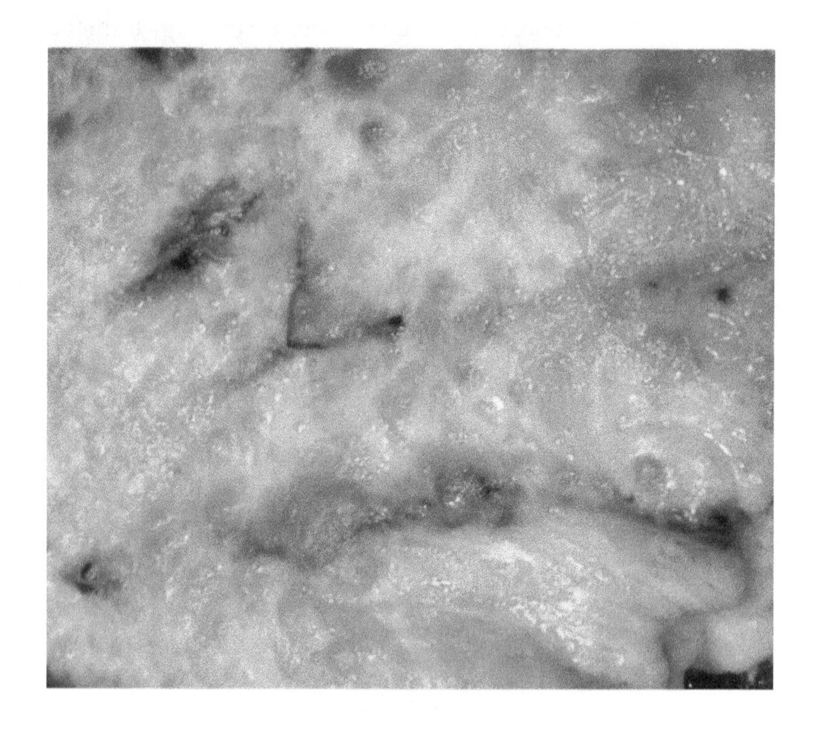

Green Chili Jack Chicken from Cracker Barrel

Try this on for size if you want some spice in your next meal. This delectable

Your taste buds will be delighted by the chicken entrée.

2 servings – 5 minutes to prepare – 20 minutes to cook

Calories 516, Total Fat 24.4 g, Carbohydrates 8.5 g, Protein 0.5 g 64.2 g protein, 697.9 mg sodium

Ingredients

- 1 pound chicken breast strips
- 1 tablespoon chili powder
- 4 oz. green chilies
- 2 cups shredded Monterey Jack cheese
- a 14 cup salsa

Preparation

- While heating some oil, season the chicken with the chili powder.
- on medium heat
- Cook the chicken strips until they are half cooked, then place them in a baking dish. the green chilies sprinkled on top of the chicken Reduce the heat to low.
- Cook for 1 to 2 minutes before topping with the cheese. Keep
- Cook the chicken and cheese together until the cheese is melted.
- Serve the chicken with the salsa on the side.

Pollo Rosa Maria from Carrabba's

If you like Carrabba's Italian Grill, you should try their pizza. Rosa Maria's Chicken Make some of this nutritious dish at home and share it with your family and friends. Share the recipe with your friends.

Serves 4 – Prep Time: 5 Minutes – Cook Time: 50 Minutes

Calories 644.4, Total Fat 52.3 g, Carbohydrates 6 g, Protein 1 g Sodium 248.2 mg, protein 36 g

Ingredients

- 4 chicken breasts, butterflied
- 4 prosciutto slices
- 4 Fontina cheese slices
- 12 CUP CLEAR BUTTER
- 3 cloves garlic
- 12 diced sweet onion
- 14 cup white wine, dry
- 4 tbsp unsweetened butter
- 12 teaspoon white pepper
- 1 teaspoon salt
- 8 ounces sliced cremini mushrooms
- 12 cup chopped fresh basil
- 1 lemon, freshly squeezed
- For garnish, use shredded Parmesan.

Preparation

- Grill the chicken breasts for 3 to 5 minutes on each side.
- Remove the chicken from the heat and stuff

it with prosciutto. as well as cheese

- On one side of the chicken, layer the ham and cheese. and then fold it over Using a toothpick, secure the filling.
- To keep the chicken warm, wrap it in foil.
- In a skillet, sauté the onions and garlic in butter until tender.
- Deglaze the pan with the white wine.
- Sauté the mushrooms in the salt, pepper, and olive oil in the same pan.
- Cook until the butter is tender, then add the remaining ingredients and continue to cook until completely combined
- Place the chicken on a plate and top with the mushroom sauce.
- it's over. Serve with the toothpick removed. Garnish with Parmesan cheese
- if desired, cheese

Chicken Pot Pie from Boston Market

This small dish is filling as well as satisfying. You can make it in under an hour a complete meal! 4 servings – 10 minutes to prepare – 40 minutes to cook

Calories 450, Total Fat 30 g, Carbohydrates 35 g, Protein 1 g Sodium 680 mg, protein 10 g

Ingredients

- 1 cup sour cream
- 1 cup chicken stock

- 3 tbsp. all-purpose flour
- 2 cups shredded skinless roasted chicken breast
- 2 cups thawed frozen mixed vegetables
- 2 tbsp chopped fresh flat-leaf parsley
- 2 tablespoons chopped chives
- 1 teaspoon chopped fresh thyme
- 1 teaspoon fresh lemon juice
- 1 teaspoon sea salt
- 12 teaspoon grated lemon zest
- 12 tsp fresh ground black pepper
- 7 ounces refrigerated pie crust, ready to use

Preparation

- Prepare by:

- Preheat the oven to 425 degrees Fahrenheit;
- Flourishing a flat surface lightly; and
- Prepare four 10-ounce ramekins.

- While stirring, bring the half-and-half, broth, and flour to a boil.

- Using a whisk
- Reduce the heat to low and continue to cook for 4 minutes.
- while still whisking the mixture
- When the mixture has thickened, stir in the remaining ingredients except for the pie crust, the mixture
- When all of the ingredients are cooked, remove from the heat and cover with a lid. the skillet Set aside the mixture while you work on the pie crust.
- Roll out the pie crust on a floured surface into a circle with a diameter of 11 inches Make a quarter-circle out of the crust.
- Fill each ramekin halfway with the warm chicken mixture.
- Cover the tops with pie crust, allowing it to hang over the edges.
- To allow the pie to cook, cut an X into each of the tops completely

- Remove the pies from the oven after 25 minutes. Allow time for rest 10 minutes before serving

Chapter 3

Recipes for Copycat Beef and Pork

Beef and Broccoli from P.F. Chang's

This healthy and tasty dish will satisfy your Asian cravings even more. With this recipe, you can prepare your favorite classic Asian dish in the comfort of your own home. your own house

Serves 4 – Prep Time: 45 Minutes – Cook Time: 15 Minutes

Calories 331, Total Fat 21.1 g, Carbohydrates 13.3 g, Protein 0.5 g 21.7 g protein, 419 mg sodium

Ingredients

- Marinade:
- 13 c. oyster sauce
- 2 tsp sesame oil, toasted
- 13 c. sherry
- 1 tablespoon soy sauce
- 1 teaspoon granulated sugar
- 1 tablespoon corn starch
- Beef with Broccoli:
- 34-pound round steak, cut into 18-inch thick strips
- three tbsp vegetable oil
- 1 fresh ginger root, thinly sliced
- 1 garlic clove, peeled and mashed
- 1-pound broccoli, peeled and cut into florets

Preparation

- In a mixing bowl, combine the marinade ingredients and stir until dissolved.
- Marinate the beef for 30 minutes in the mixture.

- For a minute, sauté the ginger and garlic in hot oil.
- When the oil has been flavored, remove the garlic and ginger and replace them. broccolini Cook the broccoli until it is tender.
- When the broccoli is done, place it in a bowl and set it aside.
- Pour the beef and marinade into the pan where you cooked it.
- Continue cooking until the beef is tender, about 5 minutes.
- Return the broccoli to the pan and cook for another 3 minutes.
- Place in a bowl or plate and serve.

Outback's Secret Steak Seasoning Mix

Steak is always a hit with the crowd. Make it just right to satisfy hungry people. Yields 3 12 tablespoons –

Prep Time: 5 Minutes – Cook Time: 10 Minutes

Calories 16.4, Total Fat 0.5 g, Carbs 3.5 g, Protein 0.5 g (spice blend only) Sodium 2328.4 mg, Protein 0.7 g

Ingredients

- Seasoning:
- 4–6 tsp sea salt
- 4 paprika teaspoons
- 2 tsp black pepper, ground
- 1 tsp onions powder
- 1 tsp. garlic powder
- 1 tsp. cayenne pepper
- 12 tsp. coriander
- 12 teaspoon of turmeric

Preparation

- In a small bowl, combine all of the seasoning ingredients. Rub the spice together. Allow resting for 15-20 minutes after blending into the meat on all sides before cooking

Chalupa from Taco Bell

Chalupas are easy to make and enjoyable to eat. Gather the ingredients and Assemble this dish with friends for a memorable dinner at home.

Serves 8 – Prep Time: 40 minutes – Cook Time: 10 minutes

Calories 424.9, Total Fat 15.8 g, Carbohydrates 47.7 g,
Protein 0.7 g 21.6 g protein, 856.8 mg sodium

Ingredients

- Tortillas:

- 212 cup flour
- 1 teaspoon baking powder
- 12 teaspoon of salt
- 1 tsp. vegetable shortening
- 1-quart milk
- For deep frying, oil
- Filling:
- a tbsp dried onion flakes
- 12 cups of water
- 1 pound minced beef
- 14 cups of flour
- 1 teaspoon chili powder
- 1 tablespoon paprika
- 1 teaspoon sea salt
- a little frying oil
- As a garnish:
- a little sour cream
- Some shredded lettuce

- Some Monterey Jack or cheddar cheese
- some diced tomato

Preparation

- In a mixing bowl, combine the flour, baking powder, and salt.
- Mix in the vegetable shortening. Then add the milk and mix well. Continue to mix.
- Cut the dough into 8 equal portions and shape them into 8 different shapes.
- Tortillas 6 in.
- Fry the tortillas in hot oil until golden brown. Cool for a few minutes.
- Begin preparing the filling. Put the onion flakes in the water and stir.
- Leave for 5 minutes.
- Combine the remaining filling ingredients (except the oil) in a mixing bowl until everything is combined
- Continue mixing after adding the onion and water.

- In a skillet, heat the oil and then cook the entire beef mixture. until the beef has browned
- Assemble your Chalupas now. Place the tortillas in a single layer.
- Layers are then added:
- Beef mixture cooked; soured cream Lettuce,
- Cheese; and finally
- Tomatoes (e)
- Place on a plate and serve.

Baby Back Ribs from Chili's

Ribs are delicious when done properly. Make and serve these ribs for a room full of happy guests at your next house party

Serves 4 – Prep Time: 15 Minutes – Cook Time: 3 Hour 30 Minutes

Calories 645, Total Fat 43.8 g, Carbohydrates 10.8 g, Protein 0.8 g 51.5 g protein, 530 mg sodium

Ingredients

- Pork:
- 4 racks baby back ribs
- Sauce:

- 112 cup water
- 1 cup distilled white vinegar
- 12 CUP TOMATO PESTO
- 1 tablespoon mustard, yellow
- 13 cup packed dark brown sugar
- 1 teaspoon liquid smoke-flavored with hickory
- 12 teaspoons of salt
- 12 tsp onion powder
- 14 tsp garlic powder
- 14 tsp. paprika

Preparation

- Bring the sauce to a boil after combining all of the ingredients.
- Reduce the sauce to a simmer once it begins to boil. Continue
- Simmer the mixture for 45-60 minutes, stirring occasionally.
- Preheat the oven to 300°F when the sauce is almost done.

- Choose a flat surface and cover it with enough aluminum foil to coat one rack of ribs Arrange the ribs on top.
- Remove the sauce from the heat and begin brushing it all over the chicken ribs.
- When the rack is completely covered, wrap it in aluminum foil.
- Place the foil on the baking pan with the opening facing upfacing the sky
- Steps 3–5 should be repeated for the remaining racks.
- Cook the ribs for 212 hours.
- Preheat your grill to medium when they're almost done baking heat.
- Grill both sides of each rack for 4 to 8 minutes. When you are almost done grilling, brush some more sauce over each side and grill for a few more minutes. Make sure that the sauce doesn't burn.
- Transfer the racks to a large plate and serve with extra sauce

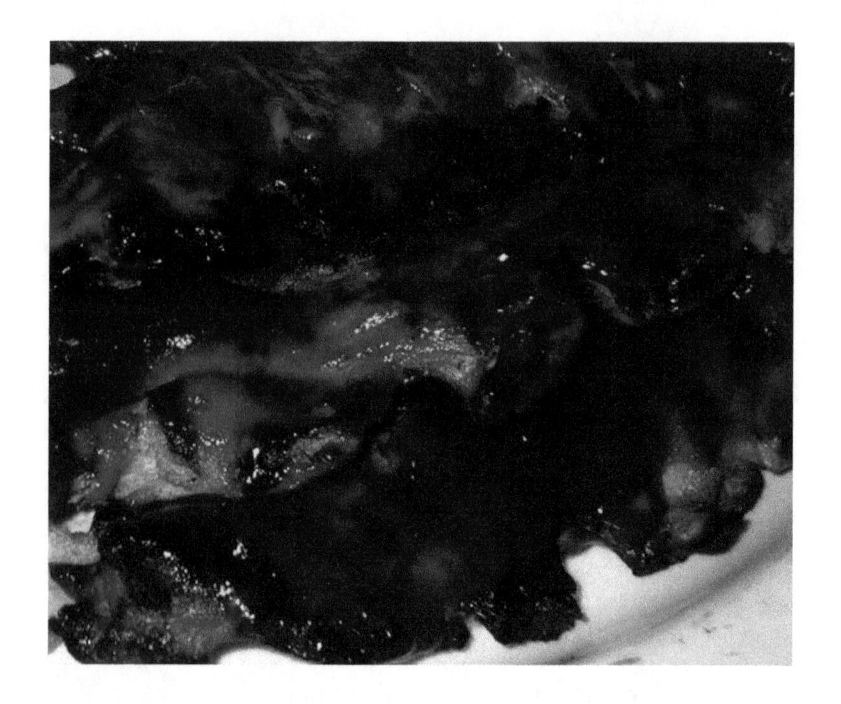

Another ribs recipe to satisfy your cravings. When they fall off the bone, you know that they are perfect.

Serves: 4 – Preparation Time: 20 minutes – Cooking Time: 3 hours 30 minutes

Nutrition facts per serving: Calories 1110, Total Fat 57 g, Carbs 89.3 g,

Protein 63 g, Sodium 3360 mg

Ingredients

- Honey Barbecue Sauce:
- 1 cup ketchup

- ½ cup corn syrup
- ½ cup honey
- ¼ cup apple cider vinegar
- ¼ cup water
- 2 tablespoons molasses
- 2 teaspoons dry mustard
- 2 teaspoons garlic powder
- 1 teaspoon chili powder
- 1 tsp onions powder
- Meat:
- 2¼ pounds pork riblets
- Salt
- Pepper
- Garlic
- ¼ teaspoon liquid smoke flavoring
- 1 teaspoon water

Preparation

- Season the riblets with salt, garlic, and pepper-based on your preferences, then sear hem on a grill until the meat starts to separate from the bone. While doing this, preheat the oven to275°F.

- Mix the water and liquid smoke flavoring into a deep pan and
- place the ribs on an elevated rack inside—make sure that the
- the liquid does not touch the ribs.
- Cover the pan with two layers of foil and bake for 2 to 5 hours, depending on the strength of your oven and the number of riblets you have. Make sure that the internal temperature of the meat reaches 155°F throughout.
- While waiting for the riblets to cook, prepare the sauce by mixing
- all of the sauce ingredients together and simmer for 20 minutes.
- When the sauce is done cooking, transfer to a bowl and set aside.
- When the ribs are done cooking, sear them on a grill until the marrow starts sizzling.

- Place the ribs on a plate and cover them generously with the sauce.
- Serve and enjoy.

Cracker Barrel's Green Beans with Bacon

This healthy meal gets a kick of flavor from the bacon. Prepare this simple yet a delicious dish to add some vegetables to your table.

Serves: 6 – Preparation Time: 10 minutes – Cooking Time: 45 minutes

Nutrition facts per serving: Calories 155.3, Total Fat 9 g, Carbs 15.7 g, Protein 6 g, Sodium 363.8 mg

Ingredients

- ¼ pound sliced bacon, cut into 1-inch pieces
- 3 cans (14.5 ounces each) green beans, with liquid

- ¼ yellow onions, peeled, chopped
- 1 teaspoon granulated sugar
- 12 teaspoon of salt
- ½ teaspoon fresh ground black pepper

Preparation

- Half-cook the bacon in a saucepan—make sure it does not get crispy.
- Add the green beans with the liquid to the browned bacon and season with salt, pepper, and sugar.
- Top the green beans with the onion and then cover the pan until the mixture boils.
- Lower the heat and allow the mixture to simmer for another 45 minutes before serving.

Café Rio's Pork

This dish goes perfectly with rice. Its tenderness and flavor will make your taste buds sing.

Serves: 10 – Preparation Time: 10 minutes – Cooking Time: 9 hours Nutrition facts per serving: Calories 317, Total Fat 7 g, Carbs 31 g, Protein 28 g, Sodium 439 mg

Ingredients

- For the Marinade:
- 3 pounds boneless pork loin
- 12 ounces Coca Cola

- ¼ cup brown sugar
- For the Seasoning:
- 1 teaspoon garlic salt
- 1 teaspoon onion salt
- 1 teaspoon chili powder
- 1 teaspoon cumin, ground
- 12 ounces Coca Cola
- For the Sauce:
- 12 ounces Coca Cola
- ¾ cup brown sugar
- ½ teaspoon chili powder
- ½ teaspoon ground cumin
- 1 can (4 ounces) green chili, ground
- 1 can (10 ounces) red enchilada sauce

Preparation

- Mix the Coca Cola and sugar in an airtight container or sealable plastic bag to make the marinade.

- Massage the marinade into the pork. Place it in the container to marinate for at least 8 hours.
- Place the pork into a slow cooker and cover with all of the seasoning ingredients in the order specified. Cook the pork on low for 7 to 9 hours.
- After cooking, shred the pork and remove the liquid from the slow cooker.
- Return the shredded pork to the slow cooker.
- Place all of the sauce ingredients in a food processor or blender.
- Blend well to create the sauce.
- Pour the sauce over the pork, and then cook the entire mixture for another 30 minutes.
- Transfer to a bowl and serve.

Ruth Chris's Filet Mignon with Béarnaise Sauce

Cooked just right, fillet mignon is one of the most delicious steaks known to man. With this simple recipe, you can make a delicious fillet mignon for dinner.

4 servings – 10 minutes to prepare – 40 minutes to cook

Nutrition facts per serving: Calories 340, Total Fat 8 g, Carbs 18 g, Protein 201 g, Sodium 580 mg

Ingredients

- Vinegar Reduction:
- 2 tablespoons tarragon vinegar
- 2 teaspoons fresh lemon juice

- 2 teaspoons shallots, finely chopped
- 1 teaspoon dried tarragon
- Fresh ground black pepper, to taste
- Sauce:
- 2 large egg yolks
- ¼ cup water
- Salt, to taste
- 2 teaspoons fresh tarragon, chopped
- 2 teaspoons fresh chervil, chopped (optional) (optional)
- ½ cup unsalted butter, melted
- Steak:
- 4 fillet mignon steaks. About 8 ounces each

Preparation

- Mix all of the vinegar reduction ingredients and bring to a boil over medium to high heat.
- When the vinegar mixture starts to boil, lower the heat and allow the mixture to simmer until most of the liquid evaporates.

- When only small bubbles of liquid are left, remove the vinegar reduction from heat and set aside.
- Bring some water to a simmer in the bottom part of a double boiler while whisking the egg yolks and water in the top part.
- Place the top part over the simmering water, making sure that the water does not touch the bottom of the bowl.
- Pour the vinegar reduction into the egg mixture and whisk until the entire mixture reaches 284°F.
- Remove the mixture from heat, but continue whisking. Slowly pour in the melted butter while continuing to whisk the mixture.
- Add in the remaining sauce ingredients and continue stirring.
- Set the Béarnaise sauce aside, keeping it warm at 220°F.
- Season the steaks with salt and pepper while preheating the broiler for 10 minutes.
- Broil the steaks to your preference (rare, medium-rare, medium well, well done).
- Transfer the steaks to a warm plate, add ¼ cup of Béarnaise sauce, and serve.

Beef and Broccoli from P.F. Chang's

This healthy and tasty dish will satisfy your Asian cravings even more. With

With this recipe, you can prepare your favorite classic Asian dish in the comfort of your own home. your own house

Serves 4 – Prep Time: 45 Minutes – Cook Time: 15 Minutes

Calories 331, Total Fat 21.1 g, Carbohydrates 13.3 g, Protein 0.5 g

21.7 g protein, 419 mg sodium

Ingredients

- Marinade:
- 13 c. oyster sauce
- 2 tsp sesame oil, toasted
- 13 c. sherry
- 1 tablespoon soy sauce
- 1 teaspoon white sugar
- 1 tablespoon corn starch
- Beef with Broccoli:
- 34 pound round steak, cut into 18-inch thick strips
- three tbsp vegetable oil

- 1 fresh ginger root, thinly sliced
- 1 garlic clove, peeled and mashed
- 1 pound broccoli, peeled and cut into florets

Preparation

- In a mixing bowl, combine the marinade ingredients and stir until dissolved.
- Marinate the beef for 30 minutes in the mixture.
- For a minute, sauté the ginger and garlic in hot
- When the oil has been flavored, remove the garlic and ginger and replace them. broccoli Cook the broccoli until it is tender.
- When the broccoli is done, place it in a bowl and set it aside.
- Pour the beef and marinade into the pan where you cooked it.
- Continue cooking until the beef is tender, about 5 minutes.
- Return the broccoli to the pan and cook for another 3 minutes.

Place in a bowl or plate and serve.

Beef and Broccoli from P.F. Chang's

This healthy and tasty dish will satisfy your Asian cravings even more. With this recipe, you can prepare your favorite classic Asian dish in the comfort of your own home your own house

Serves 4 – Prep Time: 45 Minutes – Cook Time: 15 Minutes

Calories 331, Total Fat 21.1 g, Carbohydrates 13.3 g, Protein 0.5 g 21.7 g protein, 419 mg sodium

Ingredients

- Marinade:
- 13 c. oyster sauce
- 2 tsp sesame oil, toasted
- 13 c. sherry
- 1 tablespoon soy sauce
- 1 teaspoon white sugar
- 1 tablespoon corn starch
- Beef with Broccoli:
- 34 pound round steak, cut into 18-inch thick strips
- three tbsp vegetable oil
- 1 fresh ginger root, thinly sliced
- 1 garlic clove, peeled and mashed
- 1 pound broccoli, peeled and cut into florets

Preparation

- In a mixing bowl, combine the marinade ingredients and stir until dissolved.
- Marinate the beef for 30 minutes in the mixture.
- For a minute, sauté the ginger and garlic in hot oil.

- When the oil has been flavored, remove the garlic and ginger and replace them broccoli Cook the broccoli until it is tender.
- When the broccoli is done, place it in a bowl and set it aside.
- Pour the beef and marinade into the pan where you cooked it.
- Continue cooking until the beef is tender, about 5 minutes.
- Return the broccoli to the pan and cook for another 3 minutes.
- Place in a bowl or plate and serve.
- Outback's Secret Steak Seasoning Mix
- Steak is always a hit with the crowd. Make it just right to satisfy hungry people. guests.
- Yields 3 12 tablespoons – Prep Time: 5 Minutes – Cook Time: 10 Minutes
- Calories 16.4, Total Fat 0.5 g, Carbs 3.5 g, Protein 0.5 g (spice blend only)
- Sodium 2328.4 mg, Protein 0.7 g
- Ingredients
- Seasoning:
- 4–6 tsp sea salt

- 4 paprika teaspoons
- 2 tsp black pepper, ground
- 1 tsp onions powder
- 1 tsp. garlic powder
- 1 tsp. cayenne pepper
- 12 tsp. coriander
- 12 teaspoon of turmeric
- Preparation
- In a small bowl, combine all of the seasoning ingredients. Rub the spice together.
- Allow resting for 15-20 minutes after blending into the meat on all sides before cooking

Chalupa from Taco Bell

Chalupas are easy to make and enjoyable to eat. Gather the ingredients and assemble this dish with friends for a memorable dinner at home.

Serves 8 – Prep Time: 40 minutes – Cook Time: 10 minutes

Calories 424.9, Total Fat 15.8 g, Carbohydrates 47.7 g, Protein 0.7 g 21.6 g protein, 856.8 mg sodium

Ingredients

- Tortillas:
- 212 cup flour
- 1 teaspoon baking powder
- 12 teaspoon of salt
- 1 tsp. vegetable shortening
- 1-quart milk
- For deep frying, oil
- Filling:
- a tbsp dried onion flakes
- 12 cups of water

- 1 pound minced beef
- 14 cups of flour
- 1 teaspoon chili powder
- 1 tablespoon paprika
- 1 teaspoon sea salt
- a little frying oil
- As a garnish:
- a little sour cream
- Some shredded lettuce
- Some Monterey Jack or cheddar cheese some diced tomato

Preparation

- In a mixing bowl, combine the flour, baking powder, and salt.
- Mix in the vegetable shortening. Then add the milk and mix well.
- Continue to mix.
- Cut the dough into 8 equal portions and shape them into 8 different shapes.
- Tortillas 6 in.
- Fry the tortillas in hot oil until golden brown. Cool for a few minutes.

- Begin preparing the filling. Put the onion flakes in the water and stir.
- Leave for 5 minutes.
- Combine the remaining filling ingredients (except the oil) in a mixing bowl until everything is combined
- Continue mixing after adding the onion and water.
- In a skillet, heat the oil and then cook the entire beef mixture until the beef has browned
- Assemble your Chalupas now. Place the tortillas in a single layer.
- Layers are then added:
- Beef mixture cooked; soured cream
- Lettuce, c)
- Cheese; and finally tomatoes (e)
- Place on a plate and serve.

Baby Back Ribs from Chili's

Ribs are delicious when done properly. Make and serve these ribs for a room full of happy guests at your next house party

Serves 4 – Prep Time: 15 Minutes – Cook Time: 3 Hour 30 Minutes

Calories 645, Total Fat 43.8 g, Carbohydrates 10.8 g, Protein 0.8 g 51.5 g protein, 530 mg sodium

Ingredients

- Pork:
- 4 racks baby back ribs
- Sauce:
- 112 cup water
- 1 cup distilled white vinegar
- 12 CUP TOMATO PESTO
- 1 tablespoon mustard, yellow
- 13 cup packed dark brown sugar
- 1 teaspoon liquid smoke-flavored with hickory
- 12 teaspoons of salt

- 12 tsp onion powder
-
- 14 tsp garlic powder
- 14 tsp. paprika

Preparation

- Bring the sauce to a boil after combining all of the ingredients.
- Reduce the sauce to a simmer once it begins to boil. Continue
- Simmer the mixture for 45-60 minutes, stirring occasionally.
- Preheat the oven to 300°F when the sauce is almost done.
- Choose a flat surface and cover it with enough aluminum foil to coat one rack of ribs Arrange the ribs on top.
- Remove the sauce from the heat and begin brushing it all over the chicken ribs.
- When the rack is completely covered, wrap it in aluminum foil.
- Place the foil on the baking pan with the opening facing up facing the sky

- Steps 3–5 should be repeated for the remaining racks.
- Cook the ribs for 212 hours.
- Preheat your grill to medium when they're almost done baking heat.
- Grill each rack for 4 to 8 minutes on both sides. When you're in
- When you're almost done grilling, brush some more sauce on each side and
- Grill for a few minutes longer. Make certain that the sauce does not burn.
- Place the racks on a large plate and top with extra sauce.

Riblets in Applebee's Honey Barbecue Sauce

Another recipe for ribs to satisfy your cravings. When they detach from the bone,

You are aware that they are flawless.

Serves 4 – Prep Time: 20 Minutes – Cook Time: 3 Hour 30 Minutes

Calories 1110, Total Fat 57 g, Carbohydrates 89.3 g, Protein 0.9 g Sodium 3360 mg, Protein 63 g

Ingredients

- Barbecue Sauce with Honey:
- 1-quart ketchup
- a 12 cup corn syrup
- 12 cups of honey
- 14 cc apple cider vinegar
- 14 cups of water
- 2 tbsp. of molasses
- 2 tsp dried mustard
- 2 tsp garlic powder
- 1 tablespoon chili powder
- 1 tsp onions powder
- Meat:

- 214-pound riblets de porc
- Salt
- Pepper
- Garlic
- 14 tsp liquid smoke flavoring
- a teaspoon of water

Preparation

- Season the riblets with salt, garlic, and pepper to taste preferences, then sear them on the grill until the meat begins to brown disentangle from the bone Preheat the oven to 350°F while you're at it 275°F.
- In a large saucepan, combine the water and liquid smoke flavoring.
- Place the ribs on an elevated rack inside—ensure that the rack is not too high.
- The liquid does not come into contact with the ribs.
- Bake for 2 to 5 hours, covered with two layers of foil. depending on the oven's power and the

number of riblets

- You already have. Check the internal temperature of the meat. reaches 155 degrees Fahrenheit throughout.

- While the riblets are cooking, make the sauce by combining all of the ingredients. combining all of

  the sauce ingredients and simmering for 20 minutes

- When the sauce is done, transfer it to a bowl and set it aside.

- When the ribs are done cooking, sear them on a grill until they are golden brown.

- The marrow begins to sizzle.

- Arrange the ribs on a plate and generously coat them with the sauce.

- Serve immediately and enjoy.

Green Beans with Bacon from Cracker Barrel

Bacon adds a savory note to this nutritious dish. Make this easy-to-prepare dish.

This dish is a delicious way to incorporate vegetables into your meal.

Serves 6 – Prep Time: 10 Minutes – Cook Time: 45 Minutes

Calories 155.3, Total Fat 9 g, Carbohydrates 15.7 g, Protein 0.5 g 6 g protein, 363.8 mg sodium

Ingredients

- 14 pounds sliced bacon, cut into 1-inch cubes
- 3 cans (14.5 oz. each) green beans, drained
- 14 yellow onion, peeled and diced
- 1 teaspoon sugar, granulated
- 12 teaspoon of salt
- 12 tsp freshly ground black pepper

Preparation

- Half-cook the bacon in a saucepan, being careful not to burn it.

- crispy.
- Add the green beans and liquid to the browned bacon and mix well. season with salt, pepper, and sugar to taste
- Cover the pan and cook until the green beans are tender.
- The mixture begins to boil.
- Reduce the heat to low and continue to cook the mixture for 45 minutes before serving

Pork at Café Rio

This dish pairs well with rice. Its tenderness and flavor will make your mouth water. Taste buds swoon.

Serves 10 – Prep Time: 10 Minutes – Cook Time: 9 Hours

Calories 317, Total Fat 7 g, Carbohydrates 31 g, Protein 1 g Sodium 439 mg, protein 28 g

Ingredients

- To make the marinade:
- 3 lb boneless pork loin
- 12 oz. Coca-Cola
- 14 cup granulated sugar
- For Seasoning:
- 1 tsp garlic powder
- 1 teaspoon onion seasoning
- 1 tablespoon chili powder
- 1 tsp cumin (ground)
- 12 oz. Coca-Cola

- To make the sauce:
- 12 oz. Coca-Cola
- a quarter-cup of brown sugar
- 12 tsp chili powder
- 12 teaspoon cumin powder
- 1 can (4 ounces) ground green chili
- 1 red enchilada sauce can (10 oz.)

Preparation

- In an airtight or sealable container, combine Coca-Cola and sugar.
- To make the marinade, use a plastic bag.
- Incorporate the marinade into the pork. Put it in the container.
- Allow marinating for at least 8 hours.
- Place the pork in a slow cooker and cover it with all of the ingredients seasoning ingredients in the specified order On medium heat, brown the pork.

- 7 to 9 hours on low
- After cooking, shred the pork and drain the liquid.
- The slow cooker.
- Place the shredded pork back into the slow cooker.
- In a food processor or blender, combine all of the sauce ingredients.
- To make the sauce, combine all of the ingredients in a blender and blend until smooth.
- Pour the sauce over the pork and cook the entire mixture for 10 minutes. 30 minutes more.
- Transfer to a serving bowl and serve.

Filet Mignon with Béarnaise Sauce from Ruth Chris

Filet mignon is one of the most delectable steaks known to man when cooked to perfection. man. You can make a delicious fillet mignon with this simple recipe dinner.

4 servings – 10 minutes to prepare – 40 minutes to cook

Calories 340, Total Fat 8 g, Carbohydrates 18 g, Protein 1 g 201 g protein, 580 mg sodium

Ingredients

- Vinegar Digestion:
- 2 tbsp tarragon vinaigrette
- 2 tsp freshly squeezed lemon juice
- 2 teaspoons finely chopped shallots
- 1 teaspoon tarragon (dried)
- to taste, freshly ground black pepper
- Sauce:
- 2 large yolks of eggs
- 14 cups of water
- season with salt to taste
- 2 teaspoons chopped fresh tarragon

- 2 teaspoons chopped fresh chervil (optional)
- 12 cup melted unsalted butter
- Steak:
- Four fillet mignon steaks each weighing approximately 8 ounces

Preparation

- Bring all of the vinegar reduction ingredients to a boil. a boil on medium-high heat
- When the vinegar mixture begins to boil, reduce the heat and set aside.
- Allow the mixture to simmer until the majority of the liquid has evaporated.
- Remove the vinegar when only small bubbles of liquid remain.
- Remove from the heat and set aside.
- Bring some water to a boil in the bottom of a double boiler.
- while whisking the egg yolks and water in the top part of the boiler

- Place the top section over the simmering water, ensuring that the
- The water in the bowl does not come into contact with the bowl's bottom.
- Whisk the vinegar reduction into the egg mixture until combined.
- The entire mixture reaches 284 degrees Fahrenheit.
- Remove the mixture from the heat while continuing to whisk. Slowly pour in the melted butter while continuing to whisk the mixture.
- Continue to stir in the remaining sauce ingredients.
- Set aside the Béarnaise sauce, keeping it warm at 220°F.
- While the oven is heating up, season the steaks with salt and pepper. 10 minutes under the broiler
- Broil the steaks to your liking (rare, medium-rare, or medium). excellent work).

- Place the steaks on a warm plate and top with 14 cups of Béarnaise sauce.
- Serve with the sauce.

P.F. Spare Ribs from Chang's

Asian spare ribs have a distinct flavor that is unmistakable. If you're in the mood for something Oriental, make this dish for your next meal.

Serves 2 – Prep Time: 5 Minutes – Cook Time: 25 Minutes

Calories 1344, Total Fat 77.2 g, Carbohydrates 113.2 g, Protein 1.2 g 52.5 g protein, 1557 mg sodium

Ingredients

- Sauce:
- 1-quart ketchup
- 1 cup corn syrup, light
- 12 c. hoisin sauce
- 12 cups of water
- 13 cup packed light brown sugar
- 2 tablespoons minced onions
- 1 teaspoon rice vinegar
- Ribs:

- 12–16 cups water
- a teaspoon of salt
- 1 rack spareribs (pork)
- 4 quarts of vegetable oil
- 1 tsp sesame seeds (for garnish)
- 1 tablespoon diced green onion for garnish

Preparation

- Bring the sauce to a boil by combining all of the ingredients.
- Reduce the sauce to a simmer for 5 minutes once it begins to boil.
- Place aside.
- Bring the water and salt to a boil in a large pot or Dutch oven bring to a boil While the water is heating up, clean the spare ribs. removing the extra fat
- When the water is boiling, immerse all of the ribs in it.
- Continue to boil for another 12 to 14 minutes.

Set aside after draining.

- While the ribs are cooling, heat the oil to 375 degrees Fahrenheit. Make a plate. by swathing it in a paper towel
- When the oil is hot enough, add 4 to 6 ribs and fry for 6 minutes.
-
- Step 6 should be repeated until all of the ribs are fried.
- Over medium heat, combine the fried ribs and the sauce. Simmer for at least a minute
- Serve the ribs with rice on a plate or in a bowl. Garnish seeds

Meatloaf from Boston Market

Usually, when you hear the word "meatloaf," you think of something bad. Prepare to have a good time.

Schema modification. This meatloaf will disprove all of your previous assumptions.

Serves 8 – Prep Time: 10 Minutes – Cook Time: 1 Hour 25 Minutes

Calories 210.1, Total Fat 10.9 g, Carbohydrates 8.8 g, Protein 0.8 g Sodium 446.9 mg, 18.3 g protein

Ingredients

- Sauce:
- 1-quart tomato sauce
- 112 tbsp. barbecue sauce
- 1 teaspoon sugar
- Meatloaf:
- 12 lb. lean ground sirloin
- 6 tbsp. all-purpose flour
- a quarter teaspoon of salt

- 12 tsp onion powder
- 1 tsp ground black pepper
- 1 teaspoon garlic powder

Preparation

- To begin, follow these steps:
- Preheat the oven to 400 degrees Fahrenheit; and
- Put the ground sirloin in a mixing bowl.
- Combine the sauce ingredients and bring to a simmer over medium heat.
- Heat to medium. Remove the sauce from the heat once it has begun to simmer.
- Set aside 2 tablespoons of the sauce and pour the remainder over the chicken .meat. Massage the sauce into the meat to thoroughly marinate it.
- Combine the remaining meatloaf ingredients in a mixing bowl.
- and continue mixing and kneading until the spices are evenly distributed integrated into the meat

- Wrap the meat in foil and place it in your loaf pan. Cook the
- 30 minutes with the meat mixture
- Before cutting, remove the pan from the oven and drain the fat.
- Cut the meatloaf into 8 equal pieces.
- Return the meatloaf to the oven and top with the reserved sauce.
- Return to the oven for a further 25 to 30 minutes.
- Place the meatloaf on a plate and set it aside to cool before serving.

Original Chili from Chili's

Nothing beats a hearty bowl of hot chili. Make this dish for your guests the following meal

Serves 4 – Prep Time: 30 Minutes – Cook Time: 4 to 8 Hours

Calories 400, Total Fat 28 g, Carbohydrates 14 g, Protein 1 g Sodium 1050 mg, protein 23 g

Ingredients

- Blend of Spices:
- 12 c. chili powder
- 1/8 cup salt
- 18 cup cumin powder
- 1 teaspoon paprika
- 1 teaspoon black pepper, ground
- 1 tsp. garlic powder
- 1/8 teaspoon cayenne pepper
- Chili:
- 4 pounds ground chuck for chili

- 314 cup water
- 16 oz. tomato sauce
- 12 cup chopped yellow onions
- 1 tbsp vegetable oil
- Masa Harina (Masa Harina):
- 1 cup of water
- 1 tbsp harina (masa harina)
- If desired, garnish with sliced green onions.

Preparation

- In a mixing bowl, combine all of the spice blend ingredients. Thoroughly combine and place the bowl aside
- Cook the meat in a stockpot over medium heat until it is brown.
- While the meat is cooking, thoroughly combine all of the spices. tomato sauce, water, and mix
- Bring the spice mixture to a boil with the browned meat.
- While the chili is heating up, sauté the onions in

- oil over medium heat.
- Heat to medium.
- When the chili has reached a boil and the onions have become translucent, add the
- Stir in the onions to the chili.
- Reduce the heat to low and let the chili cook for an hour.
- Every 15 minutes, stir the mixture.
- Combine the masa harina ingredients in a mixing bowl. When it comes to
- After the chili has been cooking for an hour, stir in the masa harina mixture.
- Cook for another 10 minutes after adding the chili.
- Transfer the chili to a serving bowl, garnish with green onions if desired, and serve.
-

BBQ Baby Back Ribs at Black Angus Steakhouse

If the first two rib recipes weren't enough for you, here's another.

Remember, perfection is falling-off-the-bone.

Serves 1 slab – Prep Time: 30 minutes – Cook Time: 6 to 8 hours

Calories 1500, Total Fat 30 g, Carbohydrates 108 g, Protein 2 g 14 g protein, 3540 mg sodium

Ingredients

- 1 rack of ribs (pork)
- Your preferred barbecue sauce
- To taste, onion powder
- To taste, garlic powder
- Marinade:
- 2 teaspoons kosher salt
- 2 tbsp. paprika
- 4 tbsp. granulated garlic
- 1 teaspoon onion powder

- 1 tablespoon cumin seeds
- 1 teaspoon Ancho Durkee pepper
- 2 tsp dried mustard
- 2 tsp ground black pepper
- The Rib Mop:
- 1 cup vinegar (red wine)
- 1 teaspoon garlic
- 1 cup of water
- 3 tbsp of soy sauce

Preparation

- Combine all of the marinade ingredients in a mixing bowl.
- To soak up the flavor, rub the marinade all over the ribs.
- Grill the meat for 3 to 4 hours over indirect heat at 250°F to 300°F hours. For added aroma, add soaked fruitwood to the coals.
- Ensure that the temperature remains between 250 and 300 degrees Fahrenheit for the duration

- of the experiment. the entire cooking time
- While the meat is cooking, combine the ingredients for the rib mop. in a mixing bowl
- Transfer the meat to an aluminum pan after three to four hours and use the rib mop to brush both sides.
- Cook the ribs for another hour before removing them from the oven and mop them once more Cook the ribs for another 3 to 4 minutes. hours, basting them with a mop and some barbecue sauce now and then hour.
- When the ribs are done grilling, sprinkle them with onion and pepper.
- Before wrapping them in aluminum foil, sprinkle them with garlic powder. Allow the
- Allow the ribs to rest for 30 minutes.
- Place the ribs on a plate and serve.

Mesquite Grilled Pork Chops from Texas Road House

Apples with Cinnamon

Fruit isn't usually eaten with meat. However, in this dish, the pairing is similar to in your mouth, there are fireworks.

Serves 2 – Prep Time: 40 Minutes – Cook Time: 40 Minutes

Calories 316, Total Fat 22.5 g, Carbohydrates 9.1 g, Protein 0.5 g 20.5 g protein, 7.8 mg sodium

Ingredients

- Apples with Cinnamon:
- four apples (peeled, sliced)
- 2 tablespoons melted butter
- 13 cup granulated sugar
- 2 teaspoons lemon juice
- a quarter teaspoon cinnamon
- Chop de porc:
- 2 room temperature pork loin chops with bone; 2 inches thick
- Paste:

- 2 tbsp extra-virgin olive oil
- 2 tbsp. Worcestershire sauce
- 2 teaspoons cracked black pepper
- 2 tablespoons chili powder
- 2 teaspoons garlic powder, granulated
- 2 tbsp. kosher salt
- 1 tsp cumin (ground)
- 12 teaspoon ground cinnamon
- Mesquite wood chips that have been soaked in water for at least 30 minutes

Preparation

- Cook all of the cinnamon apple ingredients together to make the apples until the apples soften in butter
- Set aside the cooked apples when they are done. Reheat before using. serving.
- Before you begin with the meat, make the following preparations:

- Soak the mesquite chips according to package directions.
- Rest the pork loin for 30 to 45 minutes at room temperature; and
- Preheat the grill to high heat.
- Mix all of the paste ingredients thoroughly. When it comes to
- When the pasta is finished, spread it over the pork chops to cover them completely.
- Take the chips out of the water and place them in an aluminum container a foil pan
- Place the pan directly over the grill's fire and cook the
- 6 minutes on both sides of the pork loin When the meat is done,
- Reduce the heat to medium after the meat has been seared.
- Cook the pork for another 25 minutes over indirect medium heat minutes.

- Remove the pork from the heat, wrap it in aluminum foil, and set it aside to rest for an additional 5 minutes
- Serve the pork with the reheated apples on a plate. Please serve the the entire dish

Chapter 4

Recipes for Copycat Fish and Seafood

Honey Grilled Salmon from Applebee's

This healthy salmon dish is something you should try.

Making it at home and tailoring it to your preferences will enhance the dish even better

Serves 4 – Prep Time: 10 Minutes – Cook Time: 30 Minutes

Calories 579.6, Total Fat 12.3 g, Carbohydrates 70.5 g, Protein 0.5 g Sodium 1515.1 mg, protein 49 g

Ingredients

- Sauce with honey and pepper:• a quarter cup honey
- 13 tbsp soy sauce
- 14 cup packed dark brown sugar
- 14 cup fresh pineapple juice
- 2 tbsp. fresh lemon juice
- 2 tbsp distilled white vinegar
- 2 tablespoons olive oil
- 1 teaspoon ground black pepper
- 12 tsp cayenne pepper
- 12 tsp. paprika
- 14 tsp garlic powder
- Fish:
- 4 salmon fillets, every 8 ounces, skinned

Preparation

- Cook until all of the sauce ingredients are combined over medium to low heat. boiling.

When the mixture begins to boil, reduce the heat slightly and set aside.

- Allow it to simmer for an additional 15 minutes.
- Grill the salmon for a few minutes after rubbing it with vegetable oil, salt, and pepper.
- 4 to 7 minutes per side
- Serve with the honey pepper sauce on the side.

Maple-Glazed Salmon and Shrimp from Red Lobster

Here's another salmon recipe, but this time Red Lobster joins forces with the delectable fish. Catch some shrimp and fish. If you enjoy Red Lobster, here is one of their most popular menu items delicious dishes

Serves 4 – Prep Time: 10 Minutes – Cook Time: 20 Minutes

Calories 364.7, Total Fat 7.4 g, Carbohydrates 38.7 g, Protein 0.7 g

34.8 g protein, 301.1 mg sodium

Ingredients

- a third cup of maple syrup
- 12 cups of water
- 2 tbsp. minced dried cherries
- 1 teaspoon sugar
- 2 tbsp. soy sauce
- 1 12 teaspoon lemon juice
- 24 pieces fresh medium peeled shrimp
- 24 oz. salmon fillets

Preparation

- To begin, follow these steps:
- Skewer the shrimp on 4 skewers (each with 6 shrimp);
- Season the shrimp with salt and pepper and set aside.
- Season the salmon generously with salt and pepper.
- Combine the maple syrup, water, cherries, sugar, soy sauce, and salt in a mixing bowl.

- Bring to a boil over medium heat with the lemon juice. lessen the
- Allow the mixture to simmer for another 8 to 10 minutes on low heat.
- Grill the shrimp for 1 to 2 minutes per side over high heat. When
- After you've finished with the shrimp, grill the salmon for 3 minutes on high heat.
- Approximately 4 minutes per side
- Place the shrimp and salmon on a plate and top with the sauce maple syrup

Garlic and Lime Shrimp from Chili's

Shrimp and garlic are excellent pairings. The addition of lime to the dish gives it a fresh taste. that extra zing and vibrancy Enjoy Chili's famous dish in the comfort of your own home.

Serves 4 – Prep Time: 5 Minutes – Cook Time: 20 Minutes

Calories 89.1, Total Fat 6.3 g, Carbohydrates 2.9 g, Protein 2.9 g 6 g protein, 725.4 mg sodium

Ingredients

- Shrimp:
- 2 tablespoons melted butter
- 1 garlic clove, chopped
- 32 peeled fresh medium shrimp
- 1 lime, cut in half
- Seasoning:
- a quarter teaspoon of salt
- 14 tsp ground black pepper
- 14 tsp cayenne pepper
- 14 tsp dried parsley flakes
- 14 tsp garlic powder
- 14 tsp. paprika
- 18 tsp dried thyme
- 18 tsp onion powder

Preparation

- To make the seasoning, combine all of the seasoning ingredients in a mixing bowl.

- For a few seconds, sauté the garlic in the butter over medium heat.
- before you add the shrimp to the pan Squeeze the lime over the salad.
- Continue to sauté the shrimp.
- Continue to sauté the mixture after adding the seasoning mix. another 5–8 minutes
- Transfer to a plate and top with thin lime wedges to serve.

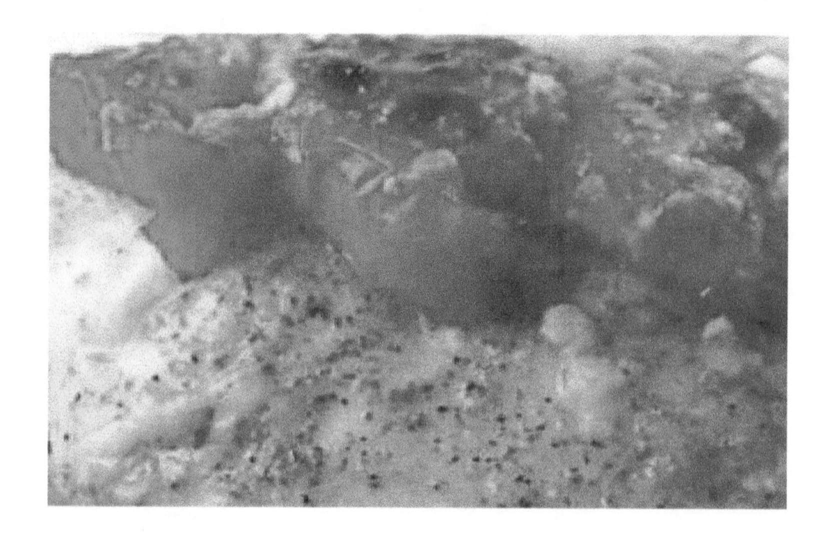

Nantucket Baked Cod at Red Lobster

Baked cod with a special spice blend is always delicious. Here's Red Lobster's menu. a variant of it We hope you have a good time with it.

Serves 4 – Prep Time: 10 Minutes – Cook Time: 30 Minutes

Calories 187.9, Total Fat 4.9 g, Carbohydrates 2.8 g, Protein 2.8 g 31.9 g protein, 303.6 mg sodium

Ingredients

- Fish:
- 4 fresh codfish fillets (approximately 1 12 pound

- 1 tablespoon melted butter
- 12 lemon juice
- 2 sliced small tomatoes
- 2 tbsp parmesan cheese, grated
- Blend of Spices:
- 14 teaspoon of salt
- 14 tsp. paprika
- 1 tsp. black pepper
- 1 teaspoon cayenne pepper

Preparation

- To begin, follow these steps:
- Preheat the oven to 450 degrees Fahrenheit; and
- Grease a 913 baking dish.
- In a mixing bowl, combine all of the spice blend ingredients thoroughly.
- Brush the tops of the cod fillets with olive oil. along with the butter

- Sprinkle the lemon juice and spice mixture over the fillets until evenly coated have used up all of the spice mixtures
- For each fish, place 2 to 3 tomato slices on top of the spices.
- Cover each tomato slice with parmesan cheese.
- Bake the fish for 8 minutes, then broil it for another 6 to 8 minutes on high.
- It takes 8 minutes.
- Place the fish in a serving dish and top with rice

Crunchy Fried Shrimp from Chili's

Chili's has mastered the art of combining protein with the perfect blend of seasonings. spices and we're passing on our knowledge to you. Make your own at home. adjusting the recipe to your preferences

Serves 8 – Prep Time: 10 Minutes – Cook Time: 1 Hour

Calories 272.9, Total Fat 8.1 g, Carbohydrates 28.7 g, Protein 0.1 g Sodium 854.2 mg, 19.3 g protein

Ingredients

- 2 pounds large peeled shrimp melted Crisco shortening crumbs made from cornflake
- Batter:

- 2/3 cup flour
- 1 13 cup cornstarch
- 12 teaspoon of salt
- 12 tsp baking powder
- six egg whites
- 13 cups of water
- four tbsp vegetable oil

Preparation

- Set aside the batter ingredients after mixing them.
- Pour the cornflake crumbs into a separate
- Preheat the oil in a medium saucepan over medium heat.
- Coat each shrimp with a generous amount of batter, then roll them in it.
- It was buried in the crumbs.
- Deep-fry the shrimp until they are golden brown.
- Place the shrimp on paper towels or oil absorbent paper.
- Serve with cocktail or tartar sauce on the side.

Garlic and Peppercorn Fried Shrimp at Applebee's

Almost every restaurant has its take on fried and breaded shrimp However; Applebee's fried shrimp is in a class of its own. Try it out and see if you can find a whole new level of delectability

Serves 4 – Prep Time: 5 Minutes – Cook Time: 30 Minutes

Calories 284.4, Total Fat 5.4 g, Carbohydrates 34 g, Protein

1 g Sodium 1021.5 mg, protein 24.4 g

Ingredients

- Shrimp:
- 1 pound peeled, deveined, and tailless shrimp
- As needed, vegetable oil
- A mixture of Flour:
- 12 cup whole wheat flour
- 14 teaspoon of salt
- 1 teaspoon black pepper, ground
- 1 teaspoon garlic granules
- 12 tsp. paprika
- 1 teaspoon sugar, granulated
- Eggs:
- 2 beaten eggs
- Breading:
- 1 pound breadcrumbs
- 1 teaspoon black pepper, ground

Preparation

- Heat 3 inches of oil to 350 degrees Fahrenheit.

- In a mixing bowl, combine the flour mixture ingredients. In
- Separately, whisk the eggs and combine the breading ingredients together.
- Dip the eggs in the flour mixture, then the eggs in the flour mixture, and finally the eggs in the flour mixture breading.
- Place the shrimp directly into the heated oil after dipping.
- 2 to 3 minutes in the oven
- Serve the cooked shrimp on a serving plate with tartar sauce or ketchup

Bang Bang Chicken and Shrimp from the Cheesecake Factory

The Cheesecake Factory creates a magical combination of Asian spices and seafood combination. If you love this dish as much as we do, then here is the recipe you've been looking for.

Serves: 4 – Preparation Time: 10 minutes – Cooking Time: 50 minutes

Nutrition facts per serving: Calories 1211, Total Fat 84.2 g, Carbs 101 g, Protein 30 g, Sodium 1940 mg

Ingredients

- Curry Sauce:
- 2 teaspoons chili oil
- ¼ cup onion
- 2 tablespoons garlic cloves, minced
- 2 teaspoons ginger
- 1 cup chicken broth
- ½ teaspoon cumin, ground
- ½ teaspoon coriander, ground
- 12 tsp. paprika
- 14 teaspoon of salt
- ¼ teaspoon black pepper, ground
- ¼ teaspoon mace, ground
- ¼ teaspoon turmeric
- 3 cups coconut milk
- 2 medium carrots, julienned
- 1 small zucchini, julienned
- ½ cup peas, frozen

- Peanut Sauce:
- ¼ cup creamy peanut butter
- 2 tablespoons water
- 4 teaspoons sugar
- 1 tablespoon soy sauce
- 1 teaspoon rice vinegar
- 1 teaspoon lime juice
- ½ teaspoon chili oil
- Protein:
- 2 chicken breast fillets, cut into bite-sized pieces
- 16 large shrimp, raw, shelled
- ¼ cup cornstarch
- ½ cup vegetable oil
- Final Dish:
- 1½ cups flaked coconut
- 4 cups white rice, cooked
- ½ teaspoon dried parsley, crumbled
- 2 tablespoons peanuts, finely chopped

- 2 green onions, julienned

Preparation

- Sauté the onion, garlic, and ginger in heated chili oil for 30 seconds before adding in the broth.
- Cook the mixture for another 30 seconds and then add in the cumin, coriander, paprika, salt, pepper, mace, and turmeric.
- Stir everything together and bring to a simmer. Keep the mixture at a simmer for 5 minutes and then add the coconut milk.
- After adding the coconut milk, bring the mixture to a boil for 20 seconds.
- Reduce the heat and then allow the mixture to simmer for 20 minutes before adding the carrots, zucchini, and peas.
- Simmer the entire mixture for another 20 minutes and set the curry sauce aside. While waiting for the mixture to thicken, preheat the oven to 300°F.
- Next, prepare the peanut sauce by mixing all of the ingredients together over medium heat.

- When the peanut sauce starts to bubble, cover the pot, remove from heat, and set aside.
- Spread the flaked coconut on a baking pan and bake for 30 minutes to toast. Swirl the flakes every 10 minutes, making sure they do not burn.
- Pour the cornstarch into a bowl. Place the prepared chicken and shrimp into the bowl and cover entirely.
- Sauté the chicken in the vegetable oil until it is cooked. Add the shrimp to the chicken and continue cooking.
- Transfer the protein to a plate and set it aside.
- Arrange the dish as follows:
- Place some rice in the center of a plate;
- Place the chicken and shrimp around the rice;
- Pour the curry sauce over the chicken and the shrimp;
- Drizzle the peanut sauce over everything—especially the rice;

- Sprinkle some parsley and peanuts over the top of the rice, then to with the onions; then
- Sprinkle the toasted coconut flakes over the dish.
- Serve and enjoy.

Disney World's Fulton's Crab House's Dungeness Crab Cakes

Disney World has amazing dishes—but you have to enter Disney World to eat them. So how about just making them in your kitchen?

Serves: 4 – Preparation Time: 15 minutes – Cooking Time: 40 minutes

Nutrition facts per serving: Calories 200, Total Fat 6 g, Carbs 18 g, Protein 18 g, Sodium 502 mg

Ingredients

- 2½ pounds Dungeness crabmeat
- 1⅛ cups unsalted soda crackers, crushed
- ⅛ cup Dijon mustard
- ½ teaspoon Old Bay Seasoning
- ⅛ cup mayonnaise
- 1 egg
- 3 tablespoons butter, melted
- 1-2 lemon, cut into thin wedges for serving
- Bearnaise sauce for serving, if desired

Preparation

- To get started:
- Squeeze the crab meat to remove moisture;
- Preheat the oven to 425°F; and
- Butter a baking sheet.
- Mix the mustard, seasoning, mayonnaise, and egg in a bowl.
- Refrigerate for 10 minutes.

- Remove the mixture from the refrigerator, and add in the cracker crumbs. Continue mixing.
- Pour the mixture over the crab and continue mixing.
- Divide the mixture into 12, and then shape each dollop into a 1- inch thick circle.
- Place the cakes on the baking sheet and drizzle some butter over each.
- Bake for 15 to 20 minutes, until cakes are cooked through. Serve with lemon wedges and bearnaise sauce, if desired.

Olive Garden's Chicken and Shrimp Carbonara

Olive Garden places a delicious twist on the simple carbonara: They add shrimp and peppers that elevate pasta's deliciousness. Here is the perfect recipe for you.

Serves: 8 – Preparation Time: 35 minutes – Cooking Time: 40 minutes

Nutrition facts per serving: Calories 1570, Total Fat 113 g, Carbs 84 g, Protein 55 g, Sodium 2400 mg

Ingredients

- Shrimp Marinade

- ¼ cup extra virgin olive oil
- ½ cup water
- 2 teaspoons Italian seasoning
- 1 tablespoon minced garlic
- Chicken
- 4 boneless and skinless chicken breasts cubed
- 1 egg mixed with 1 tablespoon cold water
- ½ cup panko bread crumbs
- ½ cup all-purpose flour
- ½ teaspoon salt
- ½ teaspoon black pepper
- 2 tablespoons olive oil
- Carbonara sauce:
- ½ cup butter (1 stick) (1 stick)
- 3 tablespoons all-purpose flour
- ½ cup parmesan cheese, grated
- 2 cups heavy cream
- cups milk

- 8 Canadian bacon slices, diced finely
- ¾ cup roasted red peppers, diced
- Pasta
- 1 teaspoon salt
- 14 ounces spaghetti or bucatini pasta (1 package) (1 package)
- Water to cook the pasta
- Shrimp
- ½ pound fresh medium shrimp, deveined and peeled
- 1-2 tablespoons olive oil for cooking

Preparation

- Mix all the marinade ingredients in a re-sealable
- container or bag and add the added shrimp. Refrigerate for at least 30 minutes.
- To make the chicken: Mix the flour, salt, pepper, and panko bread crumbs into a shallow dish. Whisk the egg with 1 tablespoon of cold water in a second shallow dish. Dip the chicken into the breadcrumb mix and after in the egg wash, and

again in the breadcrumb mix. Place on a plate and let rest until all the chicken is prepared.

- Warm the olive oil over medium heat in a deep large skillet.
- Working in batches, add the chicken. Cook for 4 to 6 minutes per side or until the chicken is cooked through. Place the cooked chicken tenders on a plate lined with paper towels to absorb excess oil.
- To make the pasta: Add water to the large pot and bring to a boil.
- Add salt and cook the pasta according to package instructions about 10-15 minutes before the sauce is ready.
- To make the shrimp: While the pasta is cooking, add olive oil to a skillet. Remove the shrimp from the marinade and shake off the excess marinade. Cook the shrimp until they turn pink, about 2-3 minutes.
- To make the Carbonara sauce: in a large deep skillet, sauté the
- Canadian bacon with a bit of butter for 3-4

minutes over medium heat or until the bacon starts to caramelize. Add the garlic and sauté for 1 minute. Remove bacon and garlic and set aside.

- In the same skillet, let the butter melt and mix in the flour.
- Gradually add the cream and milk and whisk until the sauce • thickens. Add the cheese
- Reduce the heat to a simmer and keep the mixture simmering while you prepare the rest of the ingredients.
- When you are ready to serve, add the drained pasta, bacon bits, roasted red peppers to the sauce. Stir to coat. Add pasta evenly to each serving plate. Top with some chicken and shrimp. Garnish with fresh parsley Serve with fresh shredded Romano or Parmesan cheese

Bubba Gump Shrimp Company's Cajun Shrimp

Cajun shrimp is a unique dish. If you love Bubba Gump's version, then try making this at home. It hits all the spots just right.

Serves: 4 – Preparation Time: 5 minutes – Cooking Time: 15 minutes

Nutrition facts per serving: Calories 270, Total Fat 234 g, Carbs 169 g, Protein 70 g, Sodium 2878 mg

Ingredients

- 2 teaspoons paprika
- 1 teaspoon dried thyme

- ¼ teaspoon nutmeg, ground
- ¼ teaspoon garlic powder
- ⅛ teaspoon cayenne pepper
- 1 tablespoon olive oil
- 1 pound fresh medium-sized shrimp, peeled, deveined
- Preparation
- Sauté all the ingredients (except for the shrimp) in oil for 30 seconds.
- When the ingredients have heated up, add the shrimp and continue sautéing for 2 to 3 minutes.
- When the shrimp is cooked entirely, transfer to a plate and serve.

Chapter 5

Copycat Vegetarian Recipes

Olive Garden's Stuffed Mushrooms

If you're in a healthy mood, try Olive Garden's stuffed mushrooms. If you've already tried them, then here's how you make them at home.

Serves: 6 – Preparation Time: 10 minutes – Cooking Time: 45 minutes

Nutrition facts per serving: Calories 293.1, Total Fat 20.3 g, Carbs 13.6 g, Protein 14.7 g, Sodium 618.8 mg

Ingredients

- Stuffed Mushrooms:
- 12 fresh mushrooms, washed, de-stemmed,
- 1 teaspoon flat-leaf parsley, minced

- ¼ teaspoon dry oregano
- ¼ cup + 1 tablespoon butter, divided; melted, cooled
- ¼ cup mozzarella cheese, finely grated
- Some fresh parsley for garnish
- Stuffing:
- 1 can (6 ounces) clams, drained, finely minced; save ¼ cup of juice
- 1 green onion, finely minced
- 1 egg, beaten
- ½ teaspoon garlic, minced
- ⅛ teaspoon garlic salt
- ½ cup Italian breadcrumbs
- 1 tablespoon red bell pepper, finely diced
- 2 tablespoons parmesan cheese, finely grated
- 1 tablespoon Romano cheese, finely grated
- 2 tablespoons mozzarella cheese, finely grated

Preparation

- Preheat the oven to 350°F and grease a small baking pan.
- Thoroughly mix all the stuffing ingredients EXCEPT the clam juice and the cheeses.
- When everything is blended, add in the clam juice and mix again.
- Next, add in the cheeses and continue mixing.
- Stuff each of the mushrooms with about 1½ teaspoons of the mixture.
- Pour 1 tablespoon of the batter into the baking pan and arrange the mushrooms on the pan. Then mix ¼ cup of the melted butter with the oregano and the parsley. Pour the butter mixture over the mushrooms.
- Cover the pan with a lid or foil and bake for 35–40 minutes.
- Uncover the mushrooms and sprinkle the remaining mozzarella cheese over the top.

Bake for another few minutes, until the cheese melts.

- Transfer to a serving plate. Garnish with parsley, if desired.

P.F. Chang's Spicy Green Beans

Beans are amazing, but P.F. Chang was able to elevate the bean magic by adding spices and peppers. This healthy dish is bursting with flavor.

Serves: 4 – Preparation Time: 10 minutes – Cooking Time: 10 minutes

Nutrition facts per serving: Calories 117.4, Total Fat 7.1 g, Carbs 12.4 g, Protein 3.3 g, Sodium 511.1 mg

Ingredients

- 1 pound green beans, rinsed and trimmed
- 2 tablespoons fresh ginger, grated

- 2 tablespoons garlic, minced
- 2 tablespoons cooking oil
- ¼ cup water
- Sauce:
- 2 tablespoons soy sauce
- 1 tablespoon rice vinegar
- 2 teaspoons sugar
- 2 tablespoons Szechuan peppercorn

Preparation

- Combine all the sauce ingredients in a bowl.
- Bring some water to a boil and add the green beans. Cook for 3 to 5 minutes, or until crispy.
- Sauté the garlic and ginger in the oil. When the mixture becomes aromatic, add in the green beans and cook for 2 to 3 minutes, or until soft
- Add in the sauce and continue stirring the beans.
- Serve with rice.

Chili's Black Bean

Chili's has amazing bean dishes. If you love Chili's black beans as much as we do, then here is the answer to your prayers.

Serves: 6 – Preparation Time: 5 minutes – Cooking Time: 25 minutes

Nutrition facts per serving: Calories 143.8, Total Fat 0.7 g, Carbs 25.9 g, Protein 9.5.2 g, Sodium 5.5 mg

Ingredients

- 2 cans (15.5 ounces each) black beans
- ½ teaspoon sugar
- 1 teaspoon ground cumin

- 1 teaspoon chili powder
- ½ teaspoon garlic powder
- 2 tablespoon red onion, diced finely
- ½ teaspoon fresh cilantro, minced (optional) (optional)
- ½ cup water
- Salt and black pepper to taste
- Pico de Gallo and or sour cream for garnish (optional) (optional)

Preparation

- Combine the beans, sugar, cumin, chili powder, garlic, onion, cilantro (if using), and water in a saucepan and mix well.
- Over medium-low heat, let the bean mixture simmer for about
- 20-25 minutes. Season with salt and pepper to taste.
- Remove the beans from heat and transfer them to serving bowls.

- Garnish with Pico de Gallo and/or a dollop of sour cream, if desired.

Same as In “N” Out’sAnimal Style Fries

When you need some comfort food and want to indulge, the Animal fries at

In “N” Out can certainly satisfy your cravings. They are easy to make, luscious, and so, so, so good!

Serves: 6-8 – Preparation Time: 10 minutes – Cooking Time: 30 minutes

Nutrition facts per serving: Calories 750, Total Fat 42 g, Carbs 54 g, Protein 19 g, Sodium 1105 mg

Ingredients

- 32 ounces frozen French fries
- 2 cups cheddar cheese, shredded
- 1 large onion, diced
- 2 tablespoons raw sugar
- 2 tablespoons olive oil
- 1 ½ cups mayonnaise
- ¾ cup ketchup
- ¼ cup sweet relish
- 1 ½ teaspoon white sugar
- 1 ½ teaspoon apple cider vinegar
- ½ teaspoon salt
- ½ teaspoon black pepper

Preparation

- Preheat oven to 350°F and place oven grill in the middle position.
- Place fries on a large baking sheet and bake in the oven according to package directions.

- In the meantime, warm the olive oil in a large non-stick skillet over medium heat.
- Add the onions and sauté for about 2 minutes until fragrant and soft.
- Add raw sugar and continue cooking until the onions caramelize.
- Remove from heat and set aside.
- Add the mayonnaise, ketchup, relish, white sugar, salt, and black
- pepper to a bowl and mix until well combined. Set aside.
- Once the fries are cooked, remove from heat and set the oven to broil.
- Sprinkle with the cheddar cheese over the fries and place under the broiler until the cheese melts, about 2-3 minutes.
- Place the cheese fries in serving bowls or on a plate. Include some
- Top with caramelized onions and mayonnaise sauce Serve right away.

Coleslaw from KFC

While KFC is best known for its chicken, they also serve a mean hamburger. coleslaw. We've found ourselves yearning for the vegetable dish more than once. We can count. Here's how you can pull it off.

Serves 10 – Prep Time: 15 Minutes – Cook Time: 0 Minutes

Calories 49.6, Total Fat 0.3 g, Carbohydrates 11.3 g, Protein 0.3 g 1.2 g protein, 138.3 mg sodium

Ingredients

- 8 cups finely diced cabbage

- 14 cup finely diced carrot
- 2 tablespoons minced onions
- 1 granulated sugar (13 cups)
- 12 teaspoon of salt
- 18 teaspoon black pepper
- 14 cups of milk
- 12 c. mayonnaise
- 14 cups of buttermilk
- 112 tbsp. white vinegar
- 212 tbsp. lemon juice

Preparation

- In a mixing bowl, combine the cabbage, carrots, and onions.
- In a blender or food processor, combine the remaining ingredients. and puree until smooth Pour the sauce over the cabbage mixture and toss to combine.
- Refrigerate for at least several hours before serving.

Baby Carrot from Cracker Barrel

Some argue that cooking the carrots in bacon grease negates the health benefits. We don't care about the vegetable's healthiness; they're delicious delicious!

Serves 6 – Prep Time: 5 Minutes – Cook Time: 45 Minutes

Calories 205, Total Fat 8.6 g, Carbohydrates 33.1 g, Protein 1.1 g 1.1 g protein, 577.4 mg sodium

Ingredients

- 1 teaspoon melted bacon grease
- 2 lbs. fresh baby carrots

- a little water
- 1 teaspoon sea salt
- 14 cup granulated sugar
- 14 cup melted butter
- 14 cups of honey

Preparation

- In a pot, heat the bacon grease. Place the carrots in the grease and cook until tender.
- Cook for 10 seconds. Add the carrots to a bowl and cover with water. salt.
- Bring the entire mixture to a boil over medium heat, then reduce it to low heat.
- Reduce the heat to low and leave it to simmer for another 30 to 45 minutes. The carrots should be half cooked by this point.
- Remove half of the water from the pot and replace it. Ingredients Continue to cook until the carrots are tender. Transfer to a mixing bowl and then serve

Gnocchi with Spicy Tomato and Wine Sauce from Olive Garden

This simple but spicy pasta dish is both nutritious and delicious. If you've attempted Try this recipe for Olive Garden's version.

4 servings – 10 minutes to prepare – 40 minutes to cook

Calories 285.8, Total Fat 18.9 g, Carbohydrates 12.1 g, Protein 1.1 g Sodium 476.9 mg, 8.4 g protein

Ingredients

- Sauce:

- 2 tbsp extra-virgin olive oil
- 6 garlic cloves, fresh
- 12 tsp chili flakes
- 1 cup white wine, dry
- 1 cup chicken stock
- 2 tomato cans (14.5 oz. each)
- 14 cup chopped fresh basil
- 14 cup chilled sweet creamy butter, cut into 1-inch cubes
- 12 cup freshly grated parmesan cheese
- Pasta:
- Gnocchi 1 pound
- season with salt to taste
- freshly crushed black pepper, to taste

Preparation

- Cook the olive oil, garlic, and chili flakes in a cold pan. on medium heat
- When the garlic begins to turn golden brown,

- pour in the wine.
- Bring the broth to a simmer in a saucepan.
- The broth should be halved after about 10 minutes. When that occurs,
- When this occurs, add the tomatoes and basil and allow the sauce to thicken.
- Continue to cook for another 30 minutes.
- Set the sauce aside to cool for 3 minutes after it has thickened.
- Place the sauce in a blender and add the butter after 3 minutes. as well as parmesan Set aside after puréeing everything together.
- Boil the gnocchi in a large pot to make the pasta. When it comes to
- When the pasta is done, strain it and combine it with the sauce.
- Put everything on a plate and serve.

Cheddar Cheese Fondue from Melting Pot

Here's a recipe for vegetables and fruits if you're planning to serve them for dinner. dip that will go over well with the guests

Serves 4 – Prep Time: 15 Minutes – Cook Time: 15 Minutes

Calories 320, Total Fat 21 g, Carbohydrates 7 g, Protein 1 g Sodium 473 mg, Protein 17 g

Ingredients

- 12 cup Coors Light

- 2 teaspoons minced garlic
- 2 tsp dried mustard powder
- 1 tsp Worcestershire sauce
- 6 oz. shredded or cubed medium-sharp cheddar cheese
- 2 oz. shredded or cubed Emmental Swiss cheese
- 2 tbsp. all-purpose flour

Preparation

- Combine the beer, garlic, mustard powder, and Worcestershire sauce in a mixing bowl.
- Melt everything together in the top part of a double boiler.
- Coat both kinds of cheese generously with flour.
- When the beer mixture is hot, add the cheese slowly while stirring combining with a whisk
- Transfer the smoothed-out cheese mixture to a saucepan. Serve with chopped

Sofritas from Chipotle

This simple but nutritious recipe is an excellent addition to your daily meals.

Chipotle's signature dish will undoubtedly look stunning on your table.

Serves 2 – Prep Time: 10 Minutes – Cook Time: 25 Minutes

Calories 470, Total Fat 19 g, Carbohydrates 59 g, Protein 1 g Sodium 1160 mg, protein 16 g

Ingredients

- Mexican Spice Blend:
- 12 tsp dried oregano leaves

- 2 teaspoons ground ancho chili powder
- 1 tsp cumin (ground)
- 12 teaspoon ground coriander
- 12 tsp kosher salt
- Sofritas:
- 1 tbsp avocado oil or olive oil
- 12 medium diced onion
- 2 minced garlic cloves
- 1 teaspoon minced chipotle chili in adobo sauce
- 1 tablespoon diced mild Hatch chili
- 1 tsp Mexican Spice Blend
- two tbsp tomato paste
- 1 (16 oz.) package organic extra-firm tofu, drained, dried, crumbled
- 1 cup of your preferred Mexican beer
- To taste, season with salt and black pepper.
- Tortillas and wedges of lime for garnish

Preparation

- Combine all of the Mexican Spice Mix ingredients in a container or bowl.
- Shake the plastic bag to combine the ingredients.
- For 5 minutes, sauté the onion and garlic in oil over medium heat.
- Sauté for another minute after adding the chilies and spice mix. minute.
- Cook for a minute after adding the tomato paste.
- Cook for 5 minutes more after adding the remaining ingredients.
- Adjust the seasoning with salt and pepper to taste.
- Remove the mixture from the heat, place it in a bowl, and serve.with tortillas and thin wedges of lime

Chapter 6

Recipes for Fake Burgers and Sandwiches

The Monte Cristo Sandwich at Disneyland Blue Bayou

The rich flavors of this sandwich make it unique. If you're in the mood for something sweet,

You want a Monte Cristo sandwich but don't want to drive to Disneyland to get it.

If you can't find one, here's how to make one at home.

8 servings – 10 minutes to prepare – 5 minutes to cook

Calories 305, Total Fat 17.9 g, Carbohydrates 23.7 g, Protein 2.7 g 12.2 g protein, 808 mg sodium

Ingredients

- 1 quart of oil
- Sandwich:
- 8 white bread slices
- 4 turkey slices
- 4 ham slices
- 4 Swiss cheese slices
- 1 tbsp. confectioner's sugar
- Batter:

- 13 cups of water
- ONE EGG
- a third cup all-purpose flour
- 134 tsp baking powder
- 12 teaspoon of salt
- 18 teaspoon ground black pepper

Preparation

- Heat 5 inches of oil over medium heat until it reaches 365°F.
- While the oil heats, combine the wet and dry batter ingredients. two separate bowls (egg and water; flour, baking powder, salt) as well as pepper).
- Slowly whisk the dry ingredients into the egg mixture, then add the
- Refrigerate the batter.
- Assemble the sandwiches in the following order:
- Bottom-of-the-barrel bread;
- Turkey

- Bacon;
- Cheddar;
- Ham, as well as
- Place bread on top.
- Divide the sandwiches into four pieces and secure them with a toothpick.
- Take the batter out of the refrigerator.
- Dip each sandwich in the batter, completely cover it, and set aside.
- Place immediately in hot oil to deep fry.
- Place the sandwiches on a baking sheet when the batter has turned golden brown.
- Remove the toothpicks from the plate.
- Serve the sandwiches dusted with sugar.

Copycat Burger and Sandwich Recipes

The Animal Style Burger from In and Out.

Since the beginning of time, In 'N' Out burgers have been legendary. Here's how it works: They're easy to make at home!

Serves 4 – Prep Time: 15 Minutes – Cook Time: 40 Minutes

Calories 670, Total Fat 41 g, Carbohydrates 39 g, Protein 1 g Sodium 100 mg, 37 g protein

Ingredients

- Onions Caramelized:

- two tbsp vegetable oil
- 2 large finely chopped onions
- a quarter teaspoon kosher salt
- 12 cups of water
- Sauce Extraordinaire:
- 14 c. mayonnaise
- 2 tbsp of ketchup
- 1 tbsp sweet and sour pickle relish
- 12 tsp white vinegar
- Burger:
- 2-pound ground beef chuck
- four hamburger buns
- 14 cup sliced dill pickles
- 34 cup shredded iceberg lettuce
- 4 to 8 thin tomato slices
- a pinch of freshly ground pepper
- 14 cup mustard (yellow)
- 8 oz. American cheese

Preparation

- Over medium heat, sauté the onions in the oil. The onions should be seasoned. along with the salt
- Cover the pan and stir occasionally until the onions are tender. become golden brown
- After 30 minutes, uncover the pan and continue to sauté for another 30 minutes.
- 8 minutes more. Check to see if the onions have caramelized.
- Pour the water into the pan, bring it to a boil, and remove it from the heat.
- Scrape the burnt bits from the bottom of the pan. Continue to cook the until the water has evaporated from the onions
- Put the onions in a bowl and set them aside.
- Set aside the special sauce ingredients in a bowl. aside.
- Make 8 equal portions of ground beef and shape them into balls. patties. Season both sides liberally with salt and pepper.

- On an oiled griddle, toast the split side of the hamburger buns.
- Cook for 3 minutes on one side of the patties. 3 minutes later,
- 12 teaspoon mustard on the uncooked side, then flip.
- Cook for another 2 minutes after adding a slice of cheese to the flipped patty.minutes.
- Place the patties on a plate.
- Assemble the burgers in the following order:
- The bottom bun;
- 1 tbsp. special sauce
- Pickled cucumbers;
- Lettuce
- Toasted tomato;
- Extra sauce;
- A cooked patty topped with cheese;
- Onions caramelized;

- I A cooked patty topped with cheese; and
- The top bun.
- Place the burgers in foil to store or on a plate to serve.

Big King Mushroom and Swiss Burger from Burger King

Burger King is another well-known burger restaurant. And it only takes 20 minutes to make this burger. minutes to put together!

Serves 4 – Prep Time: 15 Minutes – Cook Time: 5 Minutes

Calories 444, Total Fat 22.2 g, Carbohydrates 31.8 g, Protein 1.8 g 28.4 g protein, 1451 mg sodium

Ingredients

- Sauce aux champignons:
- 1 can condensed golden mushroom soup (1034 oz.)
- 1 can (412 ounces) sliced and drained mushrooms
- 1 tsp Worcestershire sauce
- Burger:
- 14 lb. ground beef
- 1 tsp seasoning salt
- 12 tsp ground black pepper
- 6 buns for hamburger
- 4 slices processed Swiss cheese

Preparation

- In a saucepan, combine the sauce ingredients and heat over low heat.
- Cook until step 4 by bringing the mixture to a simmer.

- Season the beef with the remaining ingredients (except the parsley). cheese), and cut into 8 equal parts. Form the portions into
- patties, and remember to stir your mushrooms while you're at it.carrying it out
- Heat a pan over medium heat and cook the patties for 3-5 minutes. minutes spent on each
- When the patties are done, place them on a plate and set them aside. removing the mushroom mixture from the heat Assemble the burgers in a pan. in this order:
- The bottom bun;
- A slice of Swiss cheese; a cooked patty
- The middle bun;
- The second patty
- 1–2 tablespoons mushroom sauce
- The top bun.
- Wrap the burgers in foil to store or serve on a plate.

Sloppy Joe from Manwich

Sloppy Joes are a favorite of both children and adults. There isn't anything to eat. arranged them neatly!

Serves 4 – Prep Time: 10 Minutes – Cook Time: 25 Minutes

Calories 323.4, Total Fat 17.4 g, Carbohydrates 19.7 g, Protein 0.7 g Sodium 1644.4 mg, protein 23.2 g

Ingredients

- 1 pound minced beef
- 1 tin (8 oz.) tomato sauce

- 1-quart ketchup
- a tbsp dried onion flakes
- 1 tablespoon finely chopped green pepper
- 1 teaspoon sea salt
- 12 teaspoon minced garlic
- 14 tsp celery seed
- 12 tsp chili powder
- 1 teaspoon dijon mustard
- four hamburger buns
- Some shredded cheese
- a few pickles
- Mustard

Preparation

- In a skillet, brown the ground beef.
- Drain the fat before adding the remaining ingredients up to the
- Toss in some hamburger buns.
- Bring the whole thing to a boil. When the

- mixture reaches a boil,
- Reduce the heat to low and leave it to simmer for another 10 minutes.
- Toast the hamburger buns while the mixture is simmering.
- Assemble the sloppy Joes in the following order:
- The bottom bun;
- Pickled cucumbers;
- Beef mash;
- Mustard powder;
- Cheddar; and
- The top bun.
- Serve immediately and enjoy.

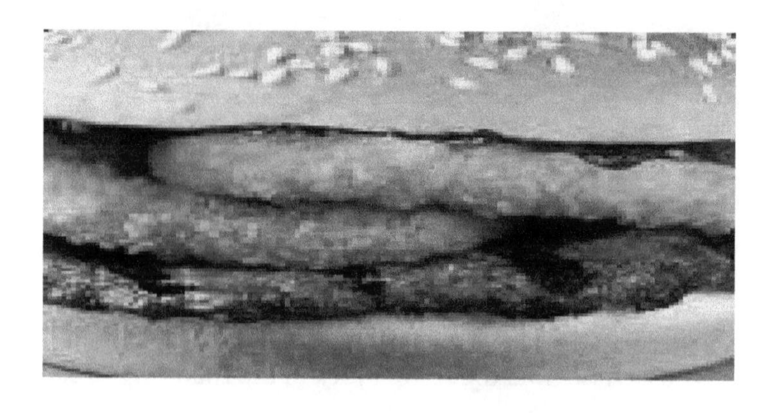

Rodeo Burger from Burger King

Here's another recipe to quench your Burger King cravings. It possesses anextra crunch that the other burger lacked

1 serving – 5 minutes to prepare – 20 minutes to cook

Calories 310, Total Fat 13 g, Carbohydrates 38 g, Protein 1 g Sodium 450 mg, 9 g protein

Ingredients

- 1 hamburger patty, fully cooked
- 1 sesame seeded hamburger bun
- 3-4 baked small onion rings
- 2 pickle slices
- 2 tablespoons BBQ sauce

Preparation

- If you're making your patty, season some ground beef with salt. and pepper, then forms into a patty.
- Fry the patty until it is fully cooked on both sides.
- Toast the buns while the patty is cooking.
- Assemble the burger as follows:
- The bottom bun;
- A patty of meat;
- Rings of onion;
- Pickled cucumbers;
- Barbecue sauce, as well as
- The top bun.
- Put the burger on a plate and serve.

The Smoke Shack Burger from Shake Shack

This item is on the Shake Shack's secret menu—some locations do not have it.

It's even available! When you crave a smoky burger, make it at home. home.

Serves 4 – Prep Time: 10 Minutes – Cook Time: 25 Minutes

Calories 620, Total Fat 42 g, Carbohydrates 26 g, Protein 1 g 35 g protein, 1602 mg sodium

Ingredients

- 12 c. mayonnaise
- 1 teaspoon Dijon mustard

- a quarter teaspoon of ketchup
- 14 tsp kosher dill pickle juice
- 1 tsp cayenne pepper
- Burger:
- 4 hamburger buns made from potatoes
- 14 cup melted unsalted butter
- 8 cooked smoked bacon slices, halved
- 12 cup diced pickled red cherry peppers
- 1 pound very cold ground beef (formed into four 1 inch thick patties)
- 1 tsp kosher salt (divided)
- 14 tsp black pepper, divided
- 4 oz. American cheese

Preparation

- Mix all of the sauce ingredients thoroughly.
- Butter the insides of the hamburger buns and toast them on a hot skillet.
- 2 to 3 minutes on the griddle

- Remove the buns and reheat the griddle for 2 to 3 minutes more. while sprinkling salt and pepper on one side of each patty
- Place the patties on the heated griddle, seasoned side down. in front of the griddle Squish the patties to 13-inch diameter with a spatula. thick.
- Season the patties' unseasoned side with salt and pepper. and cook for another 2 to 3 minutes.
- When the patty juices are bubbling, flip them and place the patties on a plate.
- Topped with cheese slices
- When the bottoms of the patties are charred, transfer them to a plate. from the griddle to the hamburger bun's bottom You can include
- If you want, put lettuce on the bun before the
- Place the cherry peppers and bacon on top of the cheese, and then top with the remaining ingredients.
- Everything comes to an end with the hamburger
- Secure the sandwich with a toothpick and serve.

Chapter 7

Olive Garden's Fettuccine Alfredo

Fettuccine Alfredo from Olive Garden

The classic Fettuccine Alfredo from Olive Garden is a simple yet elegant dish. It's

It's simple to make and delicious to eat.

Serves 6 – Prep Time: 5 Minutes – Cook Time: 25 Minutes

Calories 767.3, Total Fat 52.9 g, Carbohydrates 57.4 g, Protein 0.7 g Sodium 367 mg, Protein 17.2 g

Ingredients

- 12 cup melted butter
- two tbsp cream cheese

- 1-quart heavy cream
- 1 tsp. garlic powder
- a pinch of salt
- a pinch of black pepper
- 13 cup grated parmesan cheese
- 1 pound cooked fettuccine

Preparation

- Melt the cream cheese in a saucepan with the melted butter over medium heat.until it is soft
- Season the mixture with garlic powder after adding the heavy cream. seasoned with salt and pepper
- Reduce the heat to low and let the mixture simmer for 10 minutes.
- 15 to 20 minutes more
- Remove the pan from the heat and stir in the parmesan. Stir everything to get the cheese to melt
- Serve with the sauce over the pasta.

Shrimp Pasta from Red Lobster

Seafood and pasta are always a winning combination. Make it at home. and savor a delectable meal

Serves 4 – Prep Time: 5 Minutes – Cook Time: 30 Minutes

Calories 590, Total Fat 26 g, Carbohydrates 54 g, Protein 1 g Sodium 1500 mg, 34 g protein

Ingredients

- 8 oz. linguini/spaghetti pasta
- 13 cup virgin olive oil
- 3 cloves garlic

- 1 pound peeled and deveined shrimp
- a third of a cup of clam juice or chicken broth
- 13 c. white wine
- 1-quart heavy cream
- 12 cup freshly grated parmesan cheese
- 14 teaspoon crushed dried basil
- 14 teaspoon crushed dried oregano
- Garnish with fresh parsley and parmesan cheese

Preparation

- Prepare the pasta according to the package directions.
- Cook the garlic in hot oil over low heat until it is tender.
- Turn the heat up to medium-low and add the shrimp. When it comes to
- When the shrimp is done, place it in a separate bowl with the other ingredients garlic. Continue to cook with the remaining oil in the pan

- Bring the clam or chicken broth to a boil in the pan.
- Adjust the heat to medium and pour in the wine. Continue to cook the
- 3 minutes more with the mixture
- Reduce the heat to low while stirring the mixture and add the sour cream and cheese Continue to stir.
- Return the shrimp to the pan when the mixture thickens. add the remaining ingredients (except the pasta).
- Pour the sauce over the pasta in a mixing bowl.
- Combine all of the ingredients and serve. Garnish with parsley and serve.
- If desired, sprinkle with parmesan cheese.

Cajun Jambalaya Pasta from the Cheesecake Factory

If the previous seafood pasta wasn't quite what you were looking for, here is another option. another one that you might prefer.

4 servings – 10 minutes to prepare – 40 minutes to cook

Calories 563.9, Total Fat 13.3 g, Carbohydrates 73.8 g, Protein 7.8 g 35.9 g protein, 1457.6 mg sodium

Ingredients

- Cajun Seasoning Mix:
- 1 teaspoon ground white pepper
- 1 tsp. cayenne pepper
- 3 tablespoons salt
- 1 tablespoon paprika
- 12 tsp garlic powder
- 12 tsp onion powder
- Shrimp and chicken:
- 2 boneless, skinless chicken breasts, halved and cut into bite-sized pieces
- 12 pound large peeled and deveined shrimp
- 1 teaspoon olive oil
- Pasta:
- 5 gallons of water
- 6 oz. fettuccine
- 6 oz. fettuccine with spinach

- Jambalaya:
- 1 teaspoon olive oil
- 2 chopped medium tomatoes
- 1 medium sliced onion
- 1 sliced green bell pepper
- 1 sliced red bell pepper
- 1 sliced yellow bell pepper
- 12 cup chicken broth
- 1 teaspoon cornstarch
- 2 teaspoons white wine
- 2 tbsp arrowroot powder
- 2 teaspoons chopped fresh parsley

Preparation

- To make the Cajun seasoning blend, combine all of the ingredients.
- Prepare the seasoning. Separate the seasoning into three equal parts.

- Coat the chicken and shrimp with a third of the seasoning.
- Cook the pasta according to the package instructions.
- While the pasta is cooking, sauté the spiced chicken in heated oil. in a large frying pan
- When the chicken begins to brown, add the shrimp and Cook until the chicken is done and the shrimp are pink.
- Place the chicken and shrimp on a separate plate and set them aside.
- Warm the oil for the jambalaya in the same pan over medium heat. Combine the tomatoes, onions, peppers, and the remaining 1/3 cup of the seasoning blend Cook for 10 minutes.
- Add the chicken and cook until the vegetables are brownish-black.
- Add shrimp back into the mix.
- To deglaze the pan, add 34 cups of chicken stock. Gently

- Scrape the pan to get rid of the burnt bits. Increase the heat to high and set aside to allow the mixture to cook.
- When the broth has completely evaporated, add the remaining
- Cook for another 5 minutes with the stock.
- Reduce the heat to low and set aside the mixture to rest. heat. In a mixing bowl, combine the white wine and arrowroot until well combined. dissolves.
- Combine the mixture with the jambalaya. Reduce the heat to low and set it aside.
- Allow the mixture to simmer.
- When the jambalaya and pasta are finished, assemble the dish as follows:
- Using pasta as the first layer;
- Drizzle the jambalaya sauce over the pasta; and
- Sprinkle parsley on top of each plate.

Steak Gorgonzola from Olive Garden

Steak with gorgonzola sauce is always delicious. However, Olive Garden's pasta delivers. to a whole new level of delectability Make this simple dish at home and enjoy it.

Take it easy for a few days.

Serves 6 – Prep Time: 10 Minutes – Cook Time: 1 Hour 30 Minutes

Calories 740.5, Total Fat 27.7 g, Carbohydrates 66 g, Protein 6.6 g 54.3 g protein, 848.1 mg sodium

Ingredients

- Pasta:
- 212 pounds boneless top sirloin steaks cut into 12-inch cubes
- 1 pound cooked fettuccine or linguini
- 2 tbsp. chopped sun-dried tomatoes
- 1 tbsp balsamic vinegar glaze
- a few chopped fresh parsley leaves
- Marinade:
- 12 cup Italian salad dressing
- 1 tbsp chopped fresh rosemary
- 1 tablespoon freshly squeezed lemon juice (optional)
- Sauce with spinach and Gorgonzola:
- 4 cups trimmed baby spinach
- 2 quarts Alfredo sauce (recipe follows)
- 12 cup chopped green onion
- 6 tbsp crumbled and divided gorgonzola)

Preparation

- Set aside the pasta after it has been cooked. Combine the marinade ingredients.

  in a container that can be sealed

- For an hour, marinate the beef in the container.
- Make the Spinach Gorgonzola while the beef is marinating. sauce. In a saucepan over medium heat, heat the Alfredo sauce.
- Mix in the spinach and green onions. Allow cooking until the spinach wilts.
- 4 tablespoons Gorgonzola cheese crumbled on top of the sauce. Allow to melt and stir. Set aside the remaining 2 tablespoons
- For garnish, use cheese. Set aside and keep warm by covering with a lid.
- When the beef has finished marinating, grill each piece according to preference. your personal preference
- In a saucepan, combine the cooked pasta and Alfredo sauce, and then place on a plate

- Top the pasta with the beef and drizzle with the balsamic glaze. sun-dried tomatoes, gorgonzola crumble, and parsley leaves.
- Serve immediately and enjoy.

Copycat Alfredo Sauce from Olive Garden

Serves 4-6 people - Prep Time: 10 minutes - Cook Time: 10 minutes

Ingredients

- 6 tbsp. (1 12 stick) butter
- 1 tablespoon minced garlic
- 2 tbsp. all-purpose flour
- 12 cup milk
- 1 pound heavy cream
- 12 cup grated Parmesan cheese
- 12 cup grated Romano cheese
- White pepper and salt
- Preparation
- Melt the butter in a large saucepan over medium heat. Add
- Stir in the garlic for about a minute.
- Stir in the flour until you have a soft paste. Gradually incorporate the cream and the milk Increase the heat to medium-high and continue

to cook until

- When the sauce begins to bubble, reduce the heat to medium. Stir

  within the cheeses Continue whisking indefinitely until you achieve the desired result. the desired level of consistency Season with salt and pepper to taste.

- Turn off the heat. Serve with your preferred pasta.

Pad Thai from Noodles and Company

Make yourself a Pad Thai if you need some comfort food. This

This dish is both refreshing and delicious.

Serves 4 – Prep Time: 5 Minutes – Cook Time: 20 Minutes

Calories 830, Total Fat 18 g, Carbohydrates 151 g, Protein 1 g

1300 mg sodium, 15 g protein

Ingredients

- Sauce:
- 12 cup hot water
- 14 cup granulated sugar
- lime juice, 6 tablespoons
- 14 cup rice vinegar (approximately)
- 14 tbsp Thai fish sauce
- 2 tsp Sriracha sauce
- Thai Pad Thai:
- 12 oz. fettuccine/linguine (uncooked)
- 2 tbsp. canola oil, divided
- 12 sliced yellow onion
- 3 fresh garlic cloves minced or pressed
- 3 lightly beaten eggs
- 12 cup sliced cabbage
- 12 cup sliced mushrooms
- 1 cup sliced carrots

- 1 cup chopped broccoli
- Garnish with cilantro, sliced green onions, and lime wedges if desired.
-

Preparation

- Boiling water should be used to dissolve the sugar. When the sugar has been
- Mix in the lime juice, vinegar, fish sauce, and sugar until completely dissolved. as well as Sriracha
- Make the noodles.
- Over medium to high heat, sauté the onion in 1 tablespoon of oil.

  for one minute Sauté for 30 seconds more after adding the garlic.
- Continue to whisk the eggs into the garlic and onion mixture.
- Cook until the egg is completely cooked.
- Transfer the egg mixture to a mixing bowl and stir in the remaining oil. the same skillet

The vegetables should be sautéd.

- When the vegetables are crisp, add half of the sauce and cook for another 5 minutes. for about 1 to 3 minutes When you've achieved the desired level of consistency,
- Transfer the egg mixture and noodles to a plate to cool. serve.

Pasta di Vinci from the Cheesecake Factory

Nothing beats the combination of pasta and mushrooms. Here's some cheesecake.

Factory's Pasta Di Vinci—make as much as you want and eat as much as you want.

Serves 4 – Prep Time: 10 Minutes – Cook Time: 50 Minutes

Calories 844.9, Total Fat 35.8 g, Carbohydrates 96.5 g, Protein 0.5 g 33.9 g protein, 1400.2 mg sodium

Ingredients

- 12 chopped red onion
- 1 cup quartered mushrooms
- 2 teaspoons minced garlic
- 1 pound chicken breast, diced
- 3 tbsp. butter (divided)
- two tbsp flour
- a teaspoon of salt
- 14 oz. white wine
- 1 cup creamed chicken soup (mixed with milk)
- four tbsp heavy cream
- Chopped basil leaves for serving
- To serve, sprinkle with parmesan cheese.
- 1 pound cooked and drained penne pasta

Preparation

- 1 tablespoon of the oil is used to sauté the onion, mushrooms, and garlic. butter.

- Remove them from the butter when they are tender and place them in a bowl. . Cook the chicken in the same pan as the vegetables.
- When the chicken is done, place it in the bowl with the sauce.
- Combine the garlic, onions, and mushrooms in a mixing bowl and set aside.
- In the same pan, make a roux with the remaining
- Melt the butter in a saucepan over low to medium heat. When the roux is finished, add-in
- the mixture of salt, wine, and cream of chicken
- Ensure that the mixture does not burn.
- Allow the mixture to thicken and simmer for a few minutes. a few minutes more
- Mix in the reserved ingredients, and then transfer
- Transfer the pasta to a bowl or plate.
- Pour the sauce over the pasta and top with the parmesan cheese.
- Serve with basil.

The Mac & Cheese at Longhorn Steakhouse

Macaroni and cheese is a traditional American dish. Mac and Cheese from Longhorn Steakhouse

The cheese is out of this world. If you don't believe us, make some and try it for yourself.

Serves 10 – Prep Time: 20 Minutes – Cook Time: 20 Minutes

Calories 610, Total Fat 37 g, Carbohydrates 43 g, Protein 1 g Sodium 1210 mg, protein 26 g

Ingredients

- 1 pound cooked cavatappi pasta
- 2 tablespoons melted butter
- two tbsp flour
- 2 quarts half-and-half
- 2 ounces shredded gruyere cheese
- 8 oz. shredded white cheddar
- 2 tbsp. shredded parmesan cheese
- 4 ounces shredded fontina cheese
- smoked paprika, 1 tsp
- 4 pieces crispy crumbled bacon
- 12 cup bread crumbs (panko)

Preparation

- Cook the melted butter and flour together over medium heat to make a roux. heat.
- When the roux is done, gradually add the half-and-half, 12 cups at a time. a little at a time,

adding more as the sauce thickens

- Slowly add the remaining ingredients (except the pasta) one at a time.
- time, allowing each ingredient to fully integrate

  into the sauce. Continue to stir the mixture until everything is warm.
- Place the pasta in a greased 139 baking pan or 6 individual baking dishes.
- Pour the sauce into the baking dishes. Garnish with bacon and
- Panko bread crumbs sprinkled on top of the pasta
- Preheat the oven to 350°F and bake the pasta for 20-25 minutes. or until the breadcrumbs begin to turn golden brown.
- Allow the pasta to cool before serving.

Chapter 8

Spaghetti Fazoli's Baked Garlic

Chicken Fazoli's Baked Garlic Chicken

Fazoli has a fantastic spaghetti recipe, which you can find below. If you want to eat some pasta,

This is a fantastic dish just for you.

Serves 8 – Prep Time: 15 Minutes – Cook Time: 45 Minutes

Calories 350, Total Fat 7 g, Carbohydrates 43 g, Protein 1 g 11 g protein, 430 mg sodium

Ingredients

- Batter:
- 12 cup biscuit dough
- 2 tbsp. grated parmesan cheese
- 1 tablespoon basil
- 1 teaspoon dried oregano
- 12 tsp garlic powder
- 14 teaspoon black pepper
- Chicken:
- 2 tbsp olive oil (divided)
- 4 halved boneless chicken breasts
- 1 cup shredded mozzarella
- Pasta:
- 1-quart made-from-scratch tomato sauce
- 1 tin (28 oz.) spaghetti sauce
- 3–5 minced garlic cloves
- 3 cups shredded mozzarella cheese
- 12 oz. cooked and drained linguine
- 12 cup grated parmesan cheese

Preparation

- To begin, follow these steps:

- Preheat the oven to 350 degrees Fahrenheit;
- Preheat a skillet over medium-high heat; and
- Coat a 13x9 baking dish with 1 tablespoon olive oil.
- Thoroughly combine all of the batter ingredients. dunk the
- Indulge the chicken breasts in the batter, completely covering each.
- Brown the chicken in the remaining olive oil in a pan. on each side
- Separately, combine the tomato sauce, spaghetti sauce, and garlic. bowl.
- 13 of the pasta should cover the bottom of the pan. Spread out 14 of the
- As the second layer, sprinkle cheese over the pasta. 1 cup of the spread sauce on top of the second layer
- Step 5 should be repeated until you only have a little sauce left. Save 1 cup for the chicken, a slice of mozzarella cheese
- Put the chicken on top of everything and cover it with the sauce. the remaining sauce

- Bake the pasta for 30 minutes, then top with the remaining ingredients. melted mozzarella cheese
- Bake for another 10 minutes before slicing and serving.

Baked Ziti from Sbarro

There's no need to go to Sbarro's for your pasta fix. Make it at home and you'll be fine.

Have fun with it however you want!

Serves 8-10 – Prep Time: 5 Minutes – Cook Time: 40 Minutes

Calories 840, Total Fat 31 g, Carbohydrates 101 g, Protein 1 g Sodium 1250 mg, 40 g protein

Ingredients

- 2 pounds cooked and drained ziti pasta
- 12 pound shredded mozzarella cheese

- 1 cup garlic-and-onion-roasted-garlic-and-onion-roasted-garlic-and-onion-roasted
- Spray cooking oil
- To serve, garlic bread
- Sauce for Pasta:
- 2 lbs ricotta cheese
- 3 oz. grated Romano cheese
- 3 cups spaghetti sauce with roasted garlic and onions
- 12 tsp black pepper

Preparation

- Begin by doing the following:
- Preheat the oven to 350 degrees Fahrenheit;
- Cooking and draining the pasta as directed on the package; and
- Spray a 13x9 baking pan lightly with cooking spray.
- Mix the pasta sauce ingredients thoroughly.
- Combine the pasta sauce and the cooked ziti in a mixing bowl.
- Cover the bottom of the baking pan with spaghetti sauce.

- Place the ziti on top of the sauce and top with the cheese shredded mozzarella cheese
- Cover the pasta loosely with aluminum foil and bake for 12 to 15 minutes. , or until the cheese is completely melted and the edges of the pan are crisp.
- The pan is bubbly and golden.
- Set the oven to broil, then uncover the ziti and place it under the broiler.
- Broil for 1-2 minutes, or until the cheese is golden (optional).
- Transfer to a serving dish and top with garlic bread.

Indonesian Peanut Sauté from Noodles and Company

This delectable Thai dish has just the right amount of heat to excite your taste buds. happy. You can make this Noodles and Company recipe in your kitchen!

Serves 4 – Prep Time: 5 Minutes – Cook Time: 30 Minutes

Calories 940, Total Fat 21 g, Carbohydrates 148 g, Protein 1 g Sodium 2400 mg, protein 41 g

Ingredients

- Marinade
- 1 tbsp hot sauce, such as Sriracha

- One lime juice
- 3 garlic cloves, pressed
- 1 tablespoon minced fresh ginger
- 2 tbsp. soy sauce
- Season with salt and pepper to taste.
- Ingredients not listed
- Oil from vegetables
- 2 pounds boneless, skinless chicken, thinly sliced
- 1 (16-ounce) package linguine noodles
- 12 cup shaved carrots
- 12 cup florets broccoli
- 4-5 finely diced green onions
- 1 cup bean sprouts + some extra for garnish
- Crushed peanuts for garnish
- Garnish with fresh cilantro
- 2–3 lime wedges for garnish
- Sauce with Peanuts
- 1 cup chicken stock
- 6 tbsp. creamy peanut butter
- 2–4 teaspoons Sriracha chili sauce, depending on how spicy you like your food three tbsp honey
- 6 tbsp of soy sauce
- 3 tbsp. fresh minced ginger

- 4–5 garlic cloves, pressed or minced

Preparation

- In a mixing bowl, combine the marinade ingredients. Include the
- Allow the chicken to soak for 10-15 minutes. Take out the chicken and
- In a large sauté pan, heat 1-2 tablespoons of vegetable oil. as in a wok In a skillet, sauté the chicken in the Sriracha mixture.
- Cook the pasta until it is al dente according to the package directions. Remove
- Remove the chicken from the heat and wrap it in foil to keep it warm.
- While the pasta is cooking, prepare the peanut sauce by
- In a small saucepan over medium heat, combine all of the ingredients a low heat Continue to cook and stir the sauce until it reaches the desired consistency. 3 minutes of smoothness
- Sauté the vegetables in the same pan you used to cook the chicken. in lard Add the beansprouts last so they don't get soggy. vercooked.

- Mix in the warm chicken when the beansprouts are half cooked. and then cover the pan Reduce the heat.
- When the noodles are done, remove them from the water and set them aside.
- Place them in the sauté pan. Add the peanut sauce and stir to combine coat.
- Divide into four bowls to serve. Garnish with crushed cilantro. peanuts, as well as bean sprouts
-

Dessert Recipes That Aren't Original

Chocolate Chip Cookies from Panera Bread

Do you fancy a chocolate chip cookie for dessert? The recipe is provided below. for the cookies at Panera Bread

Serves 12 – Prep Time: 15 Minutes – Cook Time: 15 Minutes

Calories per serving: 440, Total Fat 23 g, Protein 1 g

Carbohydrates: 59 g, Protein: 4 g, Sodium: 240 mg

Ingredients

- 212 oz. unsalted butter
- 1 / 4 cup dark brown sugar

- 14 cup sugar, granulated
- 2 tsp vanilla extract
- two eggs
- 212 cup all-purpose flour
- 1 teaspoon cornstarch
- 1 tsp. baking soda
- 1 teaspoon sea salt
- 1 (12 oz.) bag mini semisweet chocolate chips

Preparation

- Using a whisk or a hand mixer, cream the butter and sugars.
- Set the wet mixture aside while you whip in the vanilla extract and eggs aside.
- In a separate bowl, combine the flour, cornstarch, and baking powder. salt and baking soda
- Pour a little of the dry mixture into the wet mixture at a time.
- Using a spatula, fold the fabric. Continue with the chocolate chips. folding.

- Form the cookie dough into balls and arrange them on a baking sheet.
- sheet. For 15 minutes, place the baking sheet in the freezer.
- While you're waiting for the cookies to bake, preheat the oven to 350°F. harden.
- Remove the frozen cookies from the freezer and place them in the oven right away. 15 minutes in the oven
-

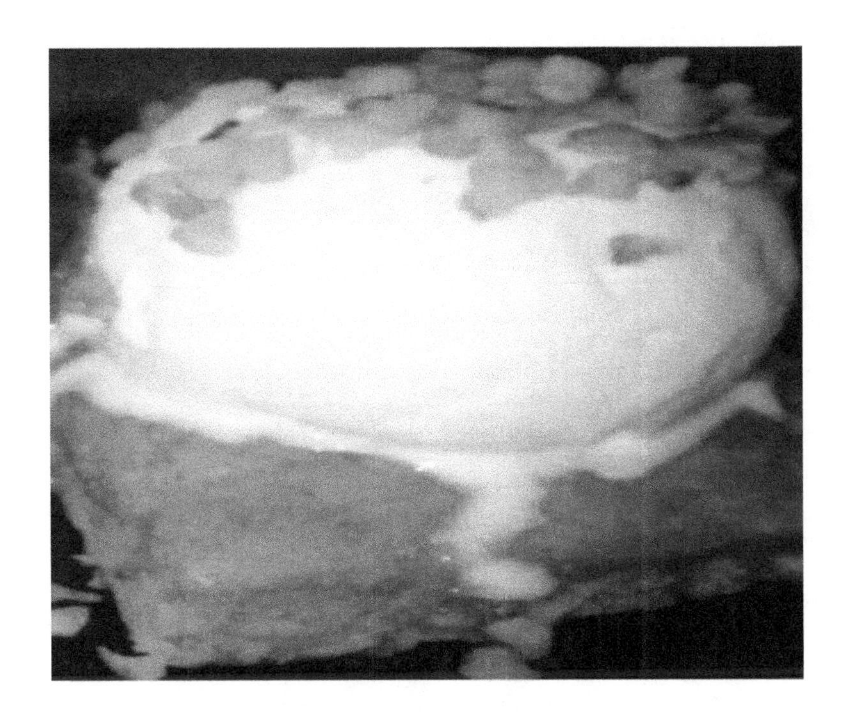

Maple Butter Blondie from Applebee's

Have a scone if you want something lighter but just as satisfying as a brownie blonde. Applebee's makes them fantastic, which is why we want you to be a part of it. capable of recreating their dish at home

Serves 6 – Prep Time: 10 Minutes – Cook Time: 25 Minutes

Calories per serving: 1000, Total Fat 54 g, Carbohydrates 117 g Sodium 620 mg, 13 g protein

Ingredients

- 13 cup melted butter
- 1 cup packed brown sugar
- 1 beaten egg
- 1 tbsp vanilla extract
- 1 cup unbleached all-purpose flour
- 12 tsp baking powder
- 18 tsp baking soda
- 18 teaspoon of salt
- 12 CUP WHITE CHOCOLATE CHIPPIES
- 12 cup chopped walnuts or pecans
- Sauce with Maple Cream:
- 12 c. maple syrup
- 14 cup melted butter
- 12 cup granulated sugar
- 8 oz. softened cream cheese
- Optional garnish: chopped walnuts
- To serve, vanilla ice cream

Preparation

- Prepare your materials as follows:
- Preheat the oven to 350 degrees Fahrenheit; and

Grease an 8-inch baking pan.

- Melt the butter and dissolve the sugar in it. Incorporate the egg and the
- Set the mixture aside and add the vanilla extract.
- In a separate bowl, combine the flour, baking powder, and baking soda as well as salt
- Pour the dry mixture slowly into the butter mixture and mix well. thoroughly.
- Before folding in, make sure the mixture is at room temperature. the almonds and chocolate chips
- Place the mixture in the baking pan and bake for 20 to 25 minutes.
- While the blondies are baking, combine the syrup and Melt the butter over low heat. After the butter has melted, add the sugar and cream cheese. Take the mixture off the heat when the cream cheese has melted, and set aside.
- Let the blondies cool a little and then cut them into rectangles.
- Serve with the syrup, top with walnuts and vanilla ice cream, if desired, and serve.

Tommy Bahama's Key Lime Pie

This refreshing dessert is the perfect end to a meal. Make some for family and friends for happy taste buds.

Serves: 2 – Preparation Time: 40 minutes – Cooking Time: 50 minutes

Nutrition facts per serving: Calories 500, Total Fat 9 g, Carbs 26 g, Protein 1 g, Sodium 110 mg

Ingredients

- Pie:
- 10-inch graham cracker crust
- 1 egg white

- 2½ cups sweetened condensed milk
- ¾ cup pasteurized egg yolk
- 1 cup lime juice
- 1 lime, zest
- 1 lime, sliced into 8
- White Chocolate Mousse Whipped Cream:
- 8 fluid ounces heavy cream
- 3 tablespoons powdered sugar
- ¼ teaspoon pure vanilla extract
- ½ tablespoon white chocolate mousse instant mix

Preparation

- Preheat the oven to 350°F while brushing the graham cracker crust with the egg white. Cover the crust completely before placing it in the oven to bake for 5 minutes.
- Whip the egg yolk and condensed milk together until they are blended completely. Add the lime juice and zest to the mixture and continue whipping until the mixture is smooth.
- If you haven't yet, remove the crust from the oven and let it cool.

- When the crust has cooled, add in the egg mixture and bake at
- 250°F for 25 to 30 minutes.
- When the pie is cooked, place it on a cooling rack to cool. Then place it in the refrigerator for at least two hours.
- While waiting for the pie to cool, beat the first three whipped cream ingredients for two minutes (if using a hand mixer) (if using a hand mixer). When the mixture is smooth, add in the chocolate mousse and beat to stiff peaks.
- Remove the pie from the refrigerator, slice it into eight pieces, and garnish each with the white chocolate mousse whipped cream and a slice of lime. Serve.

Dairy Queen's Blizzard

Dairy Queen's ice cream always hits the spot. If you're craving a Blizzard but there's no DQ in your neighborhood, here's an easy recipe that will satisfy your cravings.

Serves: 1 – Preparation Time: 5 minutes – Cooking Time: 0 minutes

Nutrition facts per serving: Calories 953, Total Fat 51.6 g, Carbs 108.8 g, Protein 15.1 g, Sodium 439.4 mg

Ingredients

- 1 candy bar, of your choice
- ¼ to ½ cup milk
- 2½ cups vanilla ice cream
- 1 teaspoon fudge sauce

Preparation

- Place the candy bar of your choice into the freezer to harden it.
- Break the candy bar into multiple tiny chunks and place all the ingredients into a blender.
- Keep blending until the ice cream becomes thicker and everything is mixed completely. our into a cup and consume.

Olive Garden's Tiramisu

This classic Italian dessert can make an ordinary meal extraordinary. If you don't know what dessert to serve, try out Olive Garden's tiramisu—you won't regret it.

Serves: 9 – Preparation Time: 10 minutes – Cooking Time: 2 hours 40 minutes

Nutrition facts per serving: Calories 288.6, Total Fat 14 g, Carbs 34.4 g, Protein 4.4 g, Sodium 53.6 mg

Ingredients

- 4 egg yolks
- 2 tablespoons milk
- ⅔ cup granulated sugar
- 2 cups mascarpone cheese
- ¼ teaspoon vanilla extract
- 1 cup heavy cream
- ½ cup cold espresso
- ¼ cup Kahlua
- 20–24 ladyfingers
- 2 teaspoons cocoa powder

Preparation

- Bring water to a boil, then reduce the heat to maintain a simmer.
- Place a heatproof bowl over the water, making sure that the bowl does not touch the water.
- In the heatproof bowl, whisk together the egg yolks, milk and sugar for about 8 to 10 minutes.
- When the mixture has thickened, remove the bowl from heat and then whisk in the vanilla and mascarpone cheese until the mixture becomes smooth

- In another bowl, whisk the cream until soft peaks are formed.
- Using a spatula, fold the whipped cream into the mascarpone
- the mixture, making sure to retain the fluffiness of the whipped cream.
- In another bowl, mix the espresso and Kahlua.
- Dip the ladyfingers into the espresso mixture one by one. Dip only the bottom, and dip them quickly so as not to make them soggy.
- Cover the bottom of an 8×8 pan with half of the dipped ladyfingers, cracking them if necessary.
- Pour half of the mascarpone mixture over the ladyfingers.
- Place another layer of ladyfingers over the mixture.
- our the rest of the mixture over the second layer of ladyfingers and smooth out the top.
- Dust some cocoa powder over the top and then place in the refrigerator.
- Slice the cake and serve when set.

Cheesecake Factory's Oreo Cheesecake

Anything with Oreo is already a must-try. But Cheesecake Factory's Oreo

Cheesecake—it's to die for. Have this simple cake at the end of your meal as a treat for your taste buds.

Serves: 10 – Preparation Time: 25 minutes – Cooking Time: 1 hour

Nutrition facts per serving: Calories 1520, Total Fat 55 g, Carbs 175 g, Protein 0 g, Sodium 736 mg

Ingredients

- Crust:
- 1½ cups Oreo cookies, crushed
- 2 tablespoons butter, melted
- Filling:
- 3 packages (8 ounces each) cream cheese, room temperature
- 1 cup sugar
- 5 large eggs, room temperature
- 2 tsp vanilla extract
- ¼ teaspoon salt
- ¼ cup all-purpose flour
- 1 container (8 ounces) sour cream, room temperature
- 14 Oreo cookies, divided

Preparation

- To make the crust, crush the whole Oreos in a blender or smash them with a rolling pin and mix them with the melted butter. Press the
- Oreo mixture to the bottom and sides of a 9-inch springform pan.

- Leave the crust to rest and preheat the oven to 325°F. Before starting to make the filling, make sure all of your ingredients are at room temperature.
- Place the cream cheese in a medium-sized bowl and beat it with a hand mixer or a whisk until it is light and fluffy.
- Beat in the sugar, mixing continuously so that the sugar is evenly distributed throughout the mixture.
- Beat in the eggs, one at a time, and then add in the vanilla, salt, and flour. When the ingredients are all mixed, add in the sour cream and 6 chopped Oreos.
- Pour the filling onto the crust and then top with 8 whole Oreos.
- Bake in the oven for an hour to an hour and 15 minutes. When the cake is done baking, leave it in the oven with the door open for an hour.
- When it has cooled down, transfer the cake to the refrigerator.
- Leave it for a day or more before serving.

TCBY's Chocolate Yogurt Pie

If you miss TCBY's healthy pies but don't want to leave your house, here's how you can stay in your humble abode while satisfying your cravings.

Serves: 2 – Preparation Time: 10 minutes – Cooking Time: 8 hours 30 minutes

Nutrition facts per serving: Calories 330, Total Fat 13 g, Carbs 49 g, Protein 4 g, Sodium 160 mg

Ingredients

- ⅔ cup butter
- 1¼ cups sugar
- 1 cup unsweetened cocoa powder

- ¼ teaspoon salt
- ½ teaspoon vanilla extract
- 2 large eggs
- ½ cup all-purpose flour
- 1-pint TCBY chocolate yogurt
- Whipped cream
- Caramel syrup

Preparation

- Before you begin, preheat the oven to 325°F.
- Place a heatproof bowl in simmering water and mix the butter, sugar, cocoa powder, and salt over the heat.
- Continue stirring and heating the mixture until it becomes
- Smooth. Remove the bowl from the heat and set it aside.
- When the mixture becomes a little cooler, mix in the vanilla extract and the eggs, one at a time. Make sure that the mixture is not too hot so that the eggs do not get cooked.
- Beat the flour into the mixture with a wooden spoon until the entire mixture is thoroughly blended.

- Transfer the mixture to a greased baking pan and then bake for
- 20 to 25 minutes.
- Remove the pie from the oven and transfer it to a cooling rack.
- When the pie has cooled down, spread frozen yogurt over the surface and freeze for 10 to 15 minutes.
- Garnish the yogurt pie with whipped cream and caramel syrup, and then return to the freezer for at least 8 hours.
- Cut the pie into equal portions and serve.

P.F. Chang's Ginger Panna Cotta

If you need to clean your palate after a heavy meal, here is a dessert that will refresh your taste buds. Thank you, P.F. Chang, for this wonderful treat.

Serves: 3 – Preparation Time: 10 minutes – Cooking Time: 4 hours 10 minutes

Nutrition facts per serving: Calories 346, Total Fat 30 g, Carbs 16 g, Protein 4 g, Sodium 50 mg

Ingredients

- Panna Cotta:
- ¼ cup heavy cream
- ½ cup granulated sugar

- 1 tablespoon grated ginger
- 1½ tablespoons powdered gelatin
- 6 tablespoons warm water
- Strawberry Sauce:
- 2 pounds ripe strawberries, hulled
- ½ cup granulated sugar
- 2 teaspoons cornstarch
- ½ lemon, juice
- 1 pinch salt

Preparation

- Place the cream, sugar, and ginger in a saucepan and cook over medium-low heat, until the sugar dissolves. Remove the mixture from heat and set aside.
- In a medium-sized bowl, mix the water and the gelatin.
- Set aside for a few minutes.
- After the gelatin has rested, pour the sugar mixture into the medium-sized bowl and stir, removing all lumps.
- Grease your ramekins and then transfer the mixture into the

- Ramekins, leaving 2 inches of space at the top.
- Place the ramekins in your refrigerator or freezer to let them set for at least 4 hours.
- While the Panna cottas are setting, make the strawberry sauce by cooking all the sauce ingredients in a medium-sized pan for 10 minutes. Stir the mixture occasionally, then remove from heat.
- When the Panna cottas are ready, flip over the containers onto a plate and allow the gelatin to stand. Drizzle with the strawberry sauce and serve.

CPSIA information can be obtained
at www.ICGtesting.com
Printed in the USA
LVHW081757160322
713569LV00003B/40